MARKETING

Official Module Guide

The Chartered Institute of Marketing
Moor Hall
Cookham
Maidenhead
Berkshire
SL6 9QH
United Kingdom

www.cim.co.uk

First published 2014

A catalogue record for this book is available from the British Library.

ISBN 978-1-9073-68-31-8 (paperback)
ISBN 978-1-907368-35-6 (ebook)

Printed and bound by Lamport Gilbert Ltd, Reading, Berkshire, RG2 0TB, UK

CONTENTS

1

MARKETING IS CONSTANTLY EVOLVING AND IT'S IMPORTANT TO DEMONSTRATE YOU HAVE KEPT UP-TO-DATE WITH THE LATEST DEVELOPMENTS.

4

Following extensive research among marketing professionals and the wider business community we recently launched a portfolio of award-based qualifications to reflect the market need for flexible bite-sized learning for today's professional marketer.

Each individual module can be achieved as a distinct self-contained award and, when combined with further awards, built into a full qualification if and when required.

Each module is based on our unique Professional Marketing Standards, designed to help you meet the ever-increasing demands on marketers at every stage of their career.

CIM (The Chartered Institute of Marketing) is the leading international professional marketing body. CIM exists to develop the marketing profession, maintain professional standards and improve the skills of marketing practitioners, enabling them to deliver exceptional results for their organisations.

Our range of professional qualifications and training programmes – along with our extensive membership benefits – are all designed to support you, develop your knowledge, enable you to grow, and increase your network. Our professional pathway will help you excel and realise your full potential.

PROFESSIONAL MARKETING STANDARDS

The Professional Marketing Standards is a framework of marketing competencies that provide a guide to the skills and behaviours expected of professional marketers at varying levels of proficiency.

Developed from extensive research with employers and employees in marketing and broader business functions, the Professional Marketing Standards give individuals and organisations the basis on which to assess the abilities of a capable and competent marketer.

More information about the Professional Marketing Standards can be found on our website: www.cim.co.uk/standards

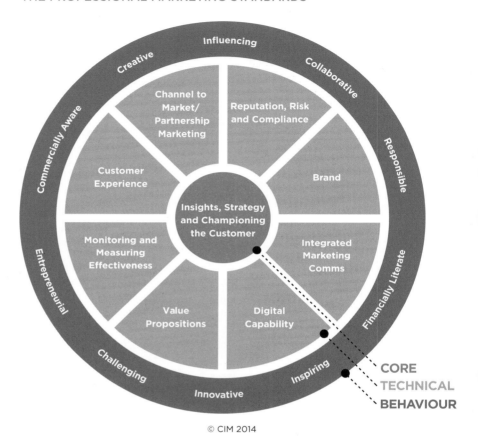

© CIM 2014

QUALIFICATION OVERVIEW

The aim of the CIM Certificate in Professional Marketing is to provide the practising marketer with relevant, contemporary marketing content to equip them for the current global landscape. Learning is brought to life through meaningful and active assessment methods that embrace the modern marketing industry.

WHAT IS THE MODULE ABOUT?

This module is designed to teach learners about the role marketing plays in delivering results in private, public and third-sector organisations. It will provide an insight into key marketing concepts and tools, explain the different theories, frameworks, models and methods of implementation and management, and demonstrate the importance of customer focus and understanding to marketing and business success.

It will also outline how external environmental factors affect planning and how information helps effective decision-making. Finally, it will introduce learners to the elements of 'the marketing mix' (or '7 Ps') and explain how to apply these to address market and customer needs.

Marketing is a 15-credit mandatory module that sits within the suite of Certificate modules. Learners will gain a module award for each individual module they pass, but to gain the CIM Certificate in Professional Marketing they need to pass both the Marketing and the mandatory Integrated Communications modules, plus one elective module – currently either Customer Experience or Digital Marketing. The choice of elective modules will be continually reviewed, and further modules may be added in line with industry demands.

MODULE CONTENT

This module comprises three units, each with two learning outcomes (see below). Each learning outcome is developed further by related assessment criteria, which are indicated by sub-headings in the text, and will be assessed through examination. You can find the module specifications within the MyCIM section of the website www.cim.co.uk

The examination will comprise 50 multiple-choice questions that learners will have to complete in a two-hour controlled assessment at the end of the module.

LEARNING OUTCOMES

The three units and six learning outcomes for this module are as follows.

1. The marketing concept
• Understand the role and function of marketing.
• Understand what influences customer behaviour.

2. Analysis and insight
• Identify factors and trends in the marketing environment and how they affect marketing planning.
• Identify options for gathering relevant marketing information.

3. Marketing mix
• Know the elements of the marketing mix
• Know how to apply and adapt the marketing mix to satisfy customer needs.

The first unit introduces some key concepts to develop learners' knowledge of what marketing is, what it can achieve and how it works within a business. It also considers a key factor within marketing – the customer and their behaviour. The customer isn't just someone who buys a product; they may also use a service, make a donation or buy into an idea or belief.

The second unit introduces the need to examine the marketing environment and identify factors, trends and changes that can have an impact on marketing and the marketing plan. It also introduces the different tools and techniques available to gather useful information from the marketing environment, which marketers can then use to make effective decisions.

The third and final unit introduces a core marketing concept – the marketing mix. The marketing mix (or '4Ps') and extended marketing mix ('7Ps') is the tactics and tools that marketers use to undertake marketing activities. The marketing mix can be used in many different ways, depending on market conditions, the information gathered, objectives and strategy, resources available, the type of business and the needs and wants of customers. Being aware of how to apply and adapt the marketing mix in different business contexts helps develop a deeper understanding of marketing.

PLANNING THE JOURNEY

You can use this workbook in the way that best suits your preferred learning style and approach to reading.

For example, you could read it from cover to cover as a course or textbook. The content within each chapter is linked and follows a logical progression.

Alternatively, you could dip into it at any point to find information and examples of key concepts and subjects. The chapters are structured around the six learning outcomes for the module and each assessment criterion is covered within the content, highlighted by sub-headings.

Each chapter contains case studies of real companies, highlighted in text boxes, which put into context the concepts and topics discussed.

There are also activities and short multiple-choice quizzes to test the knowledge you've gained while reading each chapter. For example, after the section on packaging in the Promotion section of 'The marketing mix', we recommend that you use what you've learnt in a real-life situation, such as shopping in a supermarket.

We've also included a glossary of key terms and definitions in each chapter. You're probably familiar with most of them.

ASSESSMENTS

The assessment for this module is a two-hour multiple-choice question (mcq) assessment, comprising 50 mcqs (40 stand-alone questions and two case study questions each with five related mcqs). It will cover all the learning outcomes and assessment criteria (please refer to the module specification for more detail). There are three different mcq formats used within this assessment – examples shown below:

Format 1

A question stem for which there is one correct answer and three incorrect distractors (see sample below).

Which of the following is a key element in the extended marketing mix? *(stem)*

a.	Place	*(distractor)*
b.	Product	*(distractor)*
c.	Process	*(correct answer)*
d.	Promotion	*(distractor)*

Format 2

A question stem and options to consider – there will be one correct answer and three incorrect distractors (see sample below).

Dev works for a large manufacturer producing small electric appliances such as toasters, kettles and food processors. He is currently starting the annual marketing planning cycle. The results of his analysis of the marketing environment will have a major impact on which of the following? *(stem)*

1.	The choice of strategy.	*(option)*
2.	The research undertaken.	*(option)*
3.	The setting of objectives.	*(option)*
4.	The choice of tactics.	*(option)*

a.	2, 3 and 4 only	*(distractor)*
b.	1, 2 and 3 only	*(distractor)*
c.	1, 2 and 4 only	*(distractor)*
d.	1, 3 and 4 only	*(correct answer)*

Format 3

Case study with five related mcqs. Each related mcq will be constructed in the same format as a stand-alone mcq but will specifically relate to the case study and other mcqs within the group. The purpose of this type of format is to pull together different strands of the syllabus within one scenario and test not only understanding but also the higher order skills of application and analysis (see next page).

Mira is a marketing manager at Health Fine Group, a producer of health foods and drinks. Mira is responsible for the health drinks range. She has carried out an initial audit of the organisation, its markets, main customers, competitors and the general state of the economy. She has also undertaken some market research across an extensive sample of the consumer population to find out how many people buy health-related products and how many buy things from Health Fine. The results of the market research show that an increasing number of people are buying health-related products but only a small number buy from Health Fine. Mira is concerned that awareness of Health Fine is too low and wants to increase the profile and visibility of the brand; achieving this is one of her objectives. She is now ready to develop a marketing plan for the products for which she has responsibility. *(Case study)*

1. **Which of the following would have been the least helpful to Mira in conducting her initial audit?** *(stem)*
   a. Economic value to the customer (EVC) *(correct answer)*
   b. PESTEL *(distractor)*
   c. Porter's five forces *(distractor)*
   d. SWOT *(distractor)*

2. **What type of market research did Mira undertake?**
   a. Primary and qualitative *(distractor)*
   b. Primary and quantitative *(correct answer)*
   c. Secondary and qualitative *(distractor)*
   d. Secondary and quantitative *(distractor)*

3. **Which of the following methods of data collection is Mira most likely to have used to gather the data for her research?**
   a. Focus group *(distractor)*
   b. Mystery shopping *(distractor)*
   c. Observation *(distractor)*
   d. Survey *(correct answer)*

4. **Which of the following would be the most helpful to Mira in developing her plan?**
   a. NPD process *(distractor)*
   b. SERVQUAL *(distractor)*
   c. SIC codes *(distractor)*
   d. SOSTAC® *(correct answer)*

5. **Which element of the marketing mix relates specifically to Mira's stated objective?**
   a. Place *(distractor)*
   b. Price *(distractor)*
   c. Product *(distractor)*
   d. Promotion *(correct answer)*

CORE BOOK

The core text for this module is the 7th Edition of *Principles and practice of marketing (2012)* by David Jobber and Fiona Ellis-Chadwick. The table below links the chapters in the core text to the chapters in the module guide (as far as it is possible to do so).

Module guide chapter	Core text chapter	Core text chapter title
1. The role and function of marketing	1	Marketing and the modern organisation
2. Influences on consumer behaviour	4	Understanding consumer behaviour
	5	Understanding organisational buyer behaviour
3. Influences on marketing planning	2	Marketing planning – an overview of marketing
	3	Marketing environment
	6	Understanding marketing ethics and corporate social responsibility
4. Gathering marketing information	7	Marketing research and information systems
	8	Market segmentation and positioning
5. The marketing mix	9	Branding
	10	Services marketing
	11	Product life cycle, portfolio planning and product growth strategies
	12	Developing new products
	13	Pricing
	14	Integrated marketing communications
	15	Mass marketing communications
	16	Direct marketing communications
	17	Distribution
	18	Digital marketing and social media
6. Meeting customer needs through the marketing mix	19	Analysing competitors and creating competitive advantage
	20	Competitive marketing strategy
	21	Global marketing strategy
	22	Managing marketing strategy, implementation and control

OTHER RESOURCES

This workbook is an important part of your learning, and written specifically for this module, but you should also study more widely and take advantage of the wealth of resources available to help you develop the knowledge, understanding and critical thinking skills that you need to pass the Marketing module.

No single resource will tell you everything, but using this workbook in conjunction with other material should make your learning experience complete, enjoyable and bang up to date.

CIM itself offers a variety of resources to all its members, including MyCIM, Marketing Expert, MyiLibrary, Ebsco and Emerald. You can find these at www.cim.co.uk/resources or within MyCIM (see below).

MyCIM

CIM itself offers a variety of resources to all its members, including Student Resources, Marketing Expert, MyiLibrary, Ebsco and Emerald. You can find these at www.cim.co.uk within MyCIM.

Student resources

These are guides to help you delve deeper into material that supports the six learning outcomes in this module. The links are taken from CIM material, and include links to Marketing Expert, Ebsco and Emerald as well as other resources that will help your learning journey.

Marketing Expert

Marketing Expert is an interactive platform that provides CIM members with content related to almost every marketing subject. There are clickable diagrams and models, and interactive text offering clear explanations of concepts, theories and frameworks.

MyiLibrary

The library at Moor Hall is open to all learners Monday to Friday between the hours of 9am and 5pm. For those who can't get to it, MyiLibrary is a good alternative. It allows you to read a range of marketing books on your desktop, and, in some cases, you can download them to your e-reader for seven days.

Ebsco and Emerald

Ebsco is an online database of reference material that is updated every day. It includes journals, magazines, newspapers and reports covering all aspects of marketing and business from around the world.

Members also have full access to the Emerald marketing eJournal collection. An online user guide provides a detailed list of current titles and information on how to search the collection. It also contains a range of older editions that the library has subscribed to historically.

Remember, all of this information is available via MyCIM.

Marketing news

Finally, one further way you can develop your knowledge and understanding is to keep up to date with what's going on in the real world of marketing. All members receive *Catalyst,* our magazine free, but magazines such as *Marketing*, *Campaign, Marketing Week* and *The Drum* provide a wealth of informative, insightful and fascinating information, augmented by up-to-date opinion, blogs, stories and resources on their websites. You could also follow the hundreds of publishers, marketing theorists, academics, companies, brands and agencies who post content on social media.

Or you could take advantage of *Cutting Edge*, the CIM's weekly digest of short and snappy marketing-related news items from across the sectors, available at www.cim.co.uk/cuttingedge when logged into MyCIM.

Please note: All information included in this Introduction was correct at the time of going to print. Please check the Study Connect e-newsletters for any updates or changes.

1.

THE
ROLE
AND
FUNCTION
OF
MARKETING

OUTLINE

This first chapter gives an overview of the role and function of marketing within an organisation, along with the importance of the customer. This is useful background for the next chapter, which looks in more detail at the importance of understanding customer behaviour. At the end of this chapter you will be able to:

- Define marketing.
- Explain marketing's role in business.
- Explain the function of marketing.
- Outline the marketing planning process.

DEFINITIONS

CIM defines marketing as "the management process responsible for identifying, anticipating and satisfying customer requirements profitably."

Philip Kotler, the US marketing guru, defines marketing as "a social and managerial process by which individuals and groups obtain what they need and want through creating, offering and exchanging products of value with others."

The American Marketing Association defines marketing as "the activity, set of institutions and processes for creating, communicating, delivering and exchanging offerings that have value for customers, clients, partners and society at large."

MARKETING

Marketing has existed as a concept for as long as people have traded goods with one another. But as you can see from the definitions above, the term 'marketing' means different things to different people. In this section we look at some of the different ways that people view marketing – as a management process, a business philosophy, an exchange process, a means to satisfy customer needs and as a catalyst for change.

Marketing as a management process

Communicating with customers is an important aspect of marketing, but marketing is about more than just brochures, websites and customer databases. It starts with knowing who the customer is and what he or she is looking for. This involves research, planning and pulling together all marketing activities, not just communications, to ensure that they are focused on the critical task of understanding the customer. In a business with a strong marketing orientation, the customer is the focal point for everything.

Marketing is different from sales. In sales you are usually selling what you've got – your existing products and services – although a professional salesperson will try to match their products to a customer's needs. In marketing the emphasis is on understanding what benefits customers want, and may want in the future, and then providing appropriate products and services for the salesperson to sell.

Marketing as a business philosophy

Not every organisation is marketing oriented – that is, it puts the customer and their needs at the centre of everything it does. In the past organisations tended to concentrate on the technology of the product, on sales or on the production process.

Henry Ford famously said about the cars that his company manufactured: "Customers can have any colour as long as it is black." Ford concentrated on production. The company was production oriented; indeed, it was one of the very first to use production lines, favouring efficiency and productivity over gaining greater understanding of its customers.

A product-oriented company concentrates on developing its product, believing that a good, high-quality product will sell itself. However, even the highest-quality, lowest-priced, most innovative product will struggle to gain market share if consumers don't want it, don't need it or don't even know it exists.

An organisation that is sales oriented will rely on its salespeople to sell its products. Sales targets for the week, month or year are its main focus. This can work well with very basic products, so long as salespeople are well trained and make every effort to identify ways in which their product can meet customers' needs.

However, if you've ever been persuaded to buy something you didn't really want or need, you'll appreciate that a company that relies on this technique will find it difficult to build customer loyalty. Having once been the victim of an aggressive sales technique you'll be very reluctant to return. And if you're dissatisfied with a product because it doesn't meet your needs, not only are you unlikely to recommend the company to others, you might actively advise them not to purchase from it. This applies to both products and services.

Even marketing-oriented companies sometimes use personal selling as part of their promotional activity. The difference between a sales-oriented company and a marketing-oriented company is that everyone in the marketing-oriented company puts the customer and their needs first at all times. Their mantra is 'think customer'.

Marketing as an exchange process
Marketing is concerned with trade. One person has something that someone else wants or needs. Before money was invented, farmers used to take their surplus goods to market and bartered or exchanged them for cloth to turn into clothes, or pots and utensils to cook with.

The farmer with more than enough for his family had a surplus that had a higher value to someone else. However, he gained something of value for himself in return through this mutually beneficial exchange process. These days, of course, we exchange money for goods, and companies measure the value they gain from the exchange in terms of profit – that is, the surplus funds they have after covering the costs of production and running the business. Before the Industrial Revolution the exchange of money for goods happened on only a small scale.

Marketing to satisfy customer needs
As we discussed above, marketing-oriented organisations concentrate on identifying customer needs and on finding ways to satisfy and delight them. This builds loyalty, which is important, because, obviously, the longer a customer remains with you, the more money they will spend with you. Also, over time they may become ambassadors for your products and services, referring other people to you. Developing this kind of culture is not easy – many companies seem keener on winning new customers through discounts and preferential rates than they are on keeping old ones – and it requires continuous reinforcement throughout the organisation.

Marketing as a catalyst for change

Change is difficult to achieve in organisations. It takes a long time to create a customer-focused organisation, and marketing gets involved in other changes too, which are driven by many different factors.

Organisations change their plans for a variety of reasons. There may have been a change in senior management, for example, and new personal objectives clash with the established organisational objectives. Or perhaps a change in the law means the business has to adapt its product and lose sales on a temporary basis.

This demonstrates that a mix of internal and external forces can affect the objectives an organisation sets. Let's consider these in turn.

Internal – One of the factors that has an impact on an organisation's objectives is the type of organisation it is. For example, a limited company can only operate under the purpose stated in its Memorandum of Association.

Other influences on an organisation's objectives include:

- The resources available to it (determined by its size, for example).
- In the case of a private limited company, a major shareholder may have a major influence.
- Large organisations may become complacent and not review progress against objectives.
- The attitudes and personal values of senior managers.

External – There are many external factors that can influence an organisation's plans and lead it to change its objectives. These factors may represent threats or opportunities, and the organisation will match its resources and capabilities accordingly when setting its objectives.

For example:

- Competitor activity may prompt a change in objectives, either to counter the competitor's action, or to change direction to compensate for it.
- The external environment is constantly changing, so the organisation's objectives are likely to change with it.
- Customer needs are also constantly changing, so the organisation's objectives may need to change to continue to meet those needs.

MARKETING'S ROLE IN BUSINESS

With the customer at the centre of all activity within the company, marketing should achieve its goal of making the company more successful. However, to develop long-term relationships with customers, companies need to satisfy them consistently and create real value for them.

The customer's perception of value is linked closely to the process of exchange. What will they get? Not only in terms of the product or service itself, but how it will make them feel about themselves and how their friends will view their purchase. And how much will it cost them to get it – in terms of money, time spent searching and so on?

Value for money has always been a factor in the choices customers make about the products and services they buy. But value for money is not just about cheaper prices – research has shown that individuals are often prepared to pay a little more for a better service.

Companies that are seriously considering customer needs will think about the following issues as well as price.

Information – What information might prospective purchasers need when comparing us with competitors? How can we make this information freely available? Have we considered the features of our products and services and all the additional benefits we might offer through them? For example, supermarkets often provide recipes and display them next to the ingredients on the shelves. This doesn't just give the customer ideas about what to cook for dinner, but also encourages them to buy more goods to make it.

Convenience – How can we save our prospective customers time when buying our products? Can we use technology to make it easier for them? Can we give them a choice about how we contact them? Many stores, for example, have started offering 'buy online and collect in-store' options to their customers.

CASE STUDY

Apple's iBeacon is a retail tracking facility that allows retailers to contact their customers with special offers when they are passing or close to a store. Customers may 'opt-in' to this form of contact, which gives them more convenience.

Association – What value might the customer gain from being 'associated' with our brand? For example, big-name brands are popular with teenagers, who, heavily influenced as they are by peer pressure, feel they 'fit 'in' when using them.

Added value – To make products easier to use, companies offer 'technical support' through their websites, or 'care lines' to provide information. Companies that are proactive in offering customers improved services for the same price add value to their offering because customers perceive they are genuinely interested in them.

CASE STUDY

Pampers nappies adds value to its offer through a range of information. It has carried out research into new mums' main concerns, and provides information to help address them. It also provides lots of fun ideas for mums and children.
See www.pampers.co.uk for further examples.

Marketing is also involved in creating and communicating **brand value**, and this in turn can create **shareholder value**. But while shareholders are important stakeholders for some organisations, in others, such as not-for-profit organisations, donors, beneficiaries and partners are the key stakeholders for whom marketers create value.

Marketing also carries out **research**. Organisations need to be aware of what is going on in their environment, and take this into account when planning marketing activities. They also need to keep in touch with customers and their changing needs. Marketers have to convert the research and data they gather into insights, which help to inform the business decision-making process.

In today's highly competitive marketplace, where technology enables companies to produce very similar products, the 'value' that a customer perceives in your package of benefits can determine whether they choose to buy from you or a competitor. Careful research into what customers really want or need helps you to monitor market trends and put the right package together to gain a competitive edge.

THE FUNCTION OF MARKETING

One of marketing's main functions, and some might say its key function, is that of 'bridge' between the customer and the organisation. As customer champion the marketer is the person who really understands the customer group that the organisation is targeting. The marketer then translates this understanding into action by representing the customer to all other departments and leading change within the organisation.

Marketers need to develop a marketing plan to demonstrate the role marketing will play in helping the organisation meet the objectives in its business plan. The marketing plan will have its own clear objectives, and lay down the strategy marketing will pursue to achieve them, complete with details of the marketing activities needed to do that.

Marketers then need to implement the plan. They won't necessarily carry out all the activities themselves, but they will take an active part in co-ordinating the activities that constitute the marketing mix (or '4Ps') or extended marketing mix ('7Ps'). We will look at the marketing mix in detail in Chapter 5. For now, here are some questions to consider.

Product – Which products will we continue to offer? What new products do we need to develop to meet customers' needs? Which products will we withdraw?

Price – What pricing policy should we adopt? What factors affect the way we price our products?

Promotion – Which customers are we targeting? What message do we need to communicate to them? Which promotional tools are best for this purpose and this audience? When shall we use them, how many times, and over what period? Will the result justify the amount we have to spend?

Place – Which channels will we use to get our products or services to the customer? Will we use just one, or do we need to use a combination? Which will be the most cost effective, and which will be most convenient for the customer?

People – Who will be the best customer-facing staff for us to employ? What training do they need? How can we ensure they are professional in their attitude and appearance?

Process – What processes and systems do we need to put in place to make sure that customers are satisfied?

Physical evidence – How can we ensure that the company's image is appropriate for what we are trying to achieve? What are the premises like? Do we need staff uniforms?

One of the biggest problems in implementing a marketing plan is persuading staff in departments outside of marketing that they need to change some of their policies and procedures.

Let's look at some examples.

Production department – Marketing, as we have seen, is all about giving the customer what they want. Production staff may have been accustomed to manufacturing large quantities of standard products. Because different customers may want small adjustments to the standard product, production may have to change its processes in order to make smaller quantities of customised products.

Finance department – The finance department's main focus in setting prices will probably be to meet all the costs and then add a margin for profit. Marketing, on the other hand, is about looking at a range of factors in the marketplace, and then arriving at a price. Marketers may want to spread the costs of producing a number of products across the whole range, with some contributing more to profit than others. This may not go down well with finance departments, many of which see marketing as a cost, not a source of income.

Sales department – Salespeople often work to short-term goals, aiming to achieve sales targets based on the volume or value of sales made. They may be remunerated by a combination of salary and commission to encourage them to sell more. Marketing emphasises the importance of customer satisfaction, and only selling products and services that are matched to customers' needs.

It's important that all staff are committed to a customer focus, because the success of an organisation is determined by everyone pulling together towards common objectives. Yet because most people prefer to work in a way they are comfortable with, they need to be convinced that they will derive some benefit by changing their approach. This is where **internal marketing** comes into play. This covers the activities and communication that the organisation carries out to create a 'customer-first' culture.

ACTIVITY 1

Think about your own organisation and others that you know quite well. Make notes on:

- The extent to which they carry out market and customer research and how they use that information to improve the way they meet customer requirements. For example, how have they developed products and services over the past five years? What improvements have they made in response to changing customer needs or identified customer dissatisfaction?
- How effectively they communicate customer requirements across the organisation and how well people at every level understand them.
- The way they manage quality and how well people understand the need to satisfy both internal and external customers. Are suppliers included in the 'quality chain'?
- The importance attached to customer care. Are all staff trained effectively, or is it deemed to be the responsibility of front-line staff only?
- The willingness of people within the organisation to make changes for the customer or meet specific requirements that may not be routine. What part does marketing play in facilitating this change?

All of these factors contribute to the level of market orientation an organisation has achieved.

1.4 THE MARKETING PLANNING PROCESS

As we outlined at the top of Section 1.3, the marketing planning process identifies the resources and capabilities of the organisation, matches them to opportunities in the marketplace and sets out the objectives to be achieved. It then involves developing a strategy to achieve the objectives, and a detailed plan for implementation and control.

The marketing plan is based on the broader business or corporate plan and clearly outlines what marketing will do to help the organisation meet its corporate objectives.

You will come across various planning models as you progress through your marketing studies, and we outline four of them in the table below. The plan serves many purposes, and, if done well, can make the difference between a business's success and failure.

		Methodologies		
	The Planning Journey (Wilson and Gilligan, 2002)	**MOST**	**APIC** (Kotler, 1997)	**SOSTAC®** (Smith, 1994)
Steps	Where are we now?	Mission	Analysis	Situation analysis
	Where do we want to be?	Objectives	Planning	Objectives
	How might we get there?	Strategy		Strategy
	Which way is best?	Tactics	Implementation	Tactics
				Action
	How can we ensure arrival?		Control	Control

Table 1.1 Marketing planning models

ACTIVITY 2

Does your organisation have a marketing plan? If so, see how closely its content maps to the frameworks above. Make notes on areas that you feel are strengths and any gaps or weaknesses in the framework that could be improved.

QUICK QUIZ – CHECK YOUR KNOWLEDGE

1. Which of the following statements indicates that an organisation is marketing oriented?
   a. The organisation has a marketing department.
   b. The organisation has a marketing plan.
   c. The organisation has a marketing budget.
   d. The organisation is customer focused.

2. The act of obtaining something of value from another party, and offering them something of value in return, is referred to as:
   a. Selling.
   b. Production.
   c. Exchange.
   d. Manufacturing.

3. Which of the following shows that a company is adopting the marketing concept?
   a. The sales force meet its targets.
   b. The HR department ensures that all staff are fairly paid.
   c. The managing director makes a statement to the press about the success of the company.
   d. Senior management organises the whole business to ensure it meets customers' needs.

4. The primary function of a marketing department is to:
   a. Act as a bridge between the customer and organisation, understanding and championing customers.
   b. Improve organisation performance by increasing sales, profits and market share.
   c. Effectively segment and target the market, increasing competitiveness.
   d. React to factors in the environment, ensuring that sales and profits are maintained.

(Answers: 1:d, 2:c, 3:d, 4:a)

2.
INFLUENCES ON CUSTOMER BEHAVIOUR

OUTLINE

This chapter gives an overview of the importance of customers' buying behaviour and what influences it. At the end of this chapter you will be able to:

- Discuss the importance of customer buying behaviour to marketers.
- Appraise the key influences in the consumer buying process.
- Appraise the key influences on the business-to-business buying process.
- Compare the different types of consumer and business-to-business buying behaviour.
- Explain the principle of market segmentation and how markets are segmented in practice.

DEFINITIONS

Consumer behaviour – The habits and patterns of consumers when buying and using products and services.

Consumer buying decision-making process – The process that consumers go through when making a purchase decision.

Decision-making unit – The team of people (usually in an organisation or family group) who make a buying decision.

Market segmentation – The division of the market place into distinct sub-groups or segments, each characterised by particular shared tastes and requiring a specific marketing mix.

Organisational buying decision-making process – The process that an organisation goes through when making a buying decision.

THE IMPORTANCE OF CUSTOMER BUYING BEHAVIOUR

To recap, customers are the focus of attention for market-oriented companies, which concentrate on identifying and meeting their needs in a profitable and efficient way.

Organisations that go beyond satisfying customers to delighting them create loyalty, and loyal customers spend more money and act as ambassadors for the organisation and its products and services.

CASE STUDY

US-based company Southwest Airlines reminds its staff about the importance of customers every time it pays them. Every payment is accompanied by the words 'From our customers'.

Developing a customer-focused culture requires constant reinforcement throughout the organisation, and internal marketing helps to keep everyone focused on the need to 'put the customer first'. The competitive environment encourages organisations to become more customer-focused and to seek new ways to retain customers. This has an impact on core skills. Marketing-oriented organisations need people who listen to their customers, are motivated to solve customers' problems and are keen to ensure that service standards are maintained and improved to meet and beat the competition.

Relationship marketing takes the concept of customer focus one step further, in that organisations adopting this approach develop marketing practices that encourage customer loyalty. They make every effort to keep in touch with the customer, compile huge databases of customer information and try to find ways of **establishing one-to-one relationships** with their most profitable customers. An in-depth understanding of customer behaviour allows companies to design their marketing tactics and campaigns more accurately and make them relevant and targeted to different customer groups.

ACTIVITY 3

Visit your favourite websites and identify the points that indicate customer focus. For example, how easy are they to navigate? What added value do they provide? Are there extra services, such as links to sources of helpful information?

KEY INFLUENCES ON THE CONSUMER BUYING PROCESS

Consumers purchase in response to a need – to replace an empty jar of coffee, to own a more fashionable mobile phone, to be like everyone else, and so on. You can break the buying process down into a series of steps during which the consumer gathers information and makes decisions. Marketers need to tailor communications to reach consumers at each stage of this process and use the appropriate medium or channel to reach them.

As a consumer yourself, you will probably recognise the following steps of the buying process.

Recognising the need – This may be basic, such as hunger, or, at the other end of the spectrum, wanting to look good by wearing a high fashion item. Advertising often triggers a need or a want because of the images it evokes. This is how lifestyle advertising works: consumers want to identify with the lifestyle portrayed in the advertisement, so go out and buy the products.

CASE STUDY

Nike, Coke and Apple are all examples of lifestyle brands. They don't sell sportswear, drinks and computer equipment; they market, respectively, an athletic lifestyle associated with high-achievers, fun and a trendsetting affluent lifestyle.

Searching for information – If the need is simple, like wanting the latest shade of lipstick, the following stages are completed quickly. The consumer gathers information on where the lipstick is sold and for what price, and then moves on to the main purchase decision. But if someone wants a new washing machine this stage will take longer. They will gather information on the models available, together with their benefits and disadvantages, from family, friends or work colleagues, the internet, consumer magazines, showrooms, personal salespeople and catalogues.

Manufacturers and service providers need to make sure that the information is available and clear. Branding is important because it makes the product or service easily recognisable and brands have a set of followers who will recommend them. You can't over-estimate the power of the satisfied customer, and at this stage recommendation by a person or a group whose opinion the consumer values and respects is a very strong influencer.

Evaluating the alternatives – The previous stage often reveals a number of alternatives. For example, a potential customer looking for a holiday abroad will have identified a number of different providers, and they now have to decide which best meets their needs. Understanding what customers in their target group want from a holiday is a key task for marketers, who need to communicate effectively at this stage. To help the customer differentiate between the different offers, they have to communicate the 'unique selling point' (USP) and specific benefits of their brand. So, for example, a travel agent may use brochures, personal selling and advertising to differentiate their product or service from that of their competitors.

The purchase decision – The consumer makes a decision based on their knowledge of the product or service and how well it meets their need. Companies often use sales promotion techniques ('buy one get one free', for example) to encourage purchase at this stage. Direct marketing and personal selling are also useful, depending on the complexity of the decision involved.

Post-purchase – Once they have used the service or taken delivery of the product, the customer decides how satisfied they are with it. This is an important stage for marketers because the customer may become dissatisfied at this point. Organisations have discovered that guarantees or the throwaway line from the salesperson – "Come back to us if there is a problem" – don't work. Most customers don't complain; they vote with their feet and just don't come back. They may also advise others to give you a wide berth too – and bad news travels far and fast these days. Advertising that customers see after purchase may help to remind or reassure them that they have made the right decision.

There is a whole variety of key influences on the consumer buying process but they can be categorised in two main groups:

- Those relating to the individual and their personality, motivation, beliefs and values etc.
- Social influences on the individual from the wider groupings he/she belongs to, such as social group, culture and family influences.

The table opposite explores these further.

Individual influences	
Personality	We are all different in our approach to making a buying decision and the personal traits that influence this. Some people are impulsive, some are distracted, and some might be extroverts who are attracted by products that appeal to their outgoing nature through advertising or the way the product is designed to be used.
Motivation	Individual motivation to buy varies because we all have different needs. Maslow's 'hierarchy of needs' suggests that lower-order needs for shelter and security must be fulfilled before social ones. The higher needs of self-respect and reaching potential come later. Some people make purchases such as the latest high fashion or holidays in expensive resorts in order to fulfil status needs.
Beliefs and values	Where personal values are met or matched by the company marketing the product, this can be a strong influence. One example might be people purchasing goods that they feel are more socially acceptable, such as 'energy efficient' or 'green' products.
Social influences	
Culture	The culture that people grow up in influences their values, beliefs, attitudes and behaviour, because they are steeped in that history and tradition.
Social class	Upper, middle, lower and skilled working are all examples of classes in a structured society. Marketers know that people belonging to a certain class prefer certain brands and products, whether they be holidays, cars, foods, restaurants, jewellers and so on.
Reference groups	Reference groups are influential groups that the individual interacts with, and tends to adopt or accept their norms of behaviour. The family is an obvious reference group, and individuals may make decisions that they know key members of their family would approve of.

Table 2.1 Influences on consumers' buying decisions

There are many other factors that influence people, including lifestyle, experience and perception. As with the factors described in the table above, these will have a different degree of importance for different consumers at different times. For example, consumers may act upon a recent experience, such as exposure to advertising or personal circumstances, when purchasing. The first is a controllable influence; the second is uncontrollable.

2.3

KEY INFLUENCES ON THE BUSINESS-TO-BUSINESS BUYING PROCESS

You can separate the buying process in business-to-business (sometimes called business-to-organisational) markets into the same kind of steps or stages that you do in business-to-consumer (B2C) markets. But these steps are different. However, as in B2C markets, each stage of the process is clearly identifiable and each may take time. In the case of a straight re-buy or routine purchase though, they may take place almost simultaneously.

The table below, which uses the example of a charity looking for an advertising agency, describes all the different steps in the organisational purchase decision-making process.

Stages	Detail
Recognition of problem or need	A charity recognises that it needs to raise additional funds and that advertising campaigns have been successful for similar organisations.
Diagnosis or description of need	The fundraising director explores the need with others and identifies the implications for the charity in order to work out how to address the need.
Product specification	The team draws up the charity's exact requirements (or specification)in a brief for the advertising agency, including objectives and budget.
Search for suppliers	The team reviews suppliers who work in the not-for-profit sector and asks for recommendations from other like-minded organisations.
Evaluation of suppliers	Suppliers submit proposals, tenders or bids according to the procedure laid down by the charity. The charity interviews prospective agencies and explores references before drawing up a shortlist. It will draw up a list of selection criteria to help it screen potential suppliers and make its final selection.
Selection of supplier	The charity evaluates proposals against its selection criteria. It asks the shortlisted agencies to prepare some work to test how well they and the charity will be able to work together, how accurately each agency interprets a brief and how clearly each agency can communicate with the target audience. The decision maker makes the final choice.

Stages	Detail
Contract	The charity and successful agency agree terms and conditions and the contract for the work. The charity team communicates the choice of agency to the rest of the organisation, with reasons.
Review	The charity will monitor and review the work the agency does. It will keep this information in order to help it when it's time to renew the contract or make another purchase decision when the same supplier is on the list.

Table 2.2 Different steps in the organisational purchase decision-making process

Many organisations have preferred lists of suppliers, which simplifies what can otherwise be a cumbersome and time-consuming decision-making process. Clients always have to strike a balance between making the right decision in the time available and considering all the options. The monitoring and review process means that at least you can take suppliers off the list who don't come up to scratch.

ACTIVITY 4

If your organisation has a purchase and supply department, talk to them to find out what criteria they use to select appropriate suppliers.

If not, list the criteria you would like a printing firm that supplies you with marketing fliers, to meet.

2.4 CONSUMER AND BUSINESS-TO-BUSINESS BUYING BEHAVIOUR COMPARED

Differences exist between consumer and business-to-business (B2B) markets in terms of:

- The number and nature of decision makers involved.
- The balance of the elements of the promotional mix.
- The message content.
- The lead time for decisions.
- The use of segmentation and research.
- Budget allocation.
- Evaluation and measurement.

The most important differences are the promotional mix, the information buyers need, the segmentation methods and the nature of the marketing message.

In business-to business-markets advertising is usually the least effective form of communication, though it may play a supporting role. The main element of the mix in many B2B markets is personal selling because, although expensive, it suits the complexity of the typical B2B decision-making processes. For example, it enables the supplier to address each customer's needs individually and encourages the development of long-term relationships.

The relatively few number of buyers and the ease of finding information about them makes direct marketing another effective mechanism. Also, editorial coverage in trade publications can be used to build awareness, provide information and create leads, opening the door for the salesperson.

Table 2.3 overleaf shows the contrast in emphasis in the use of the communications mix.

Market	Communication mix
Business to business	Personal selling
	Exhibitions
	Trade advertising
	Websites
	LinkedIn
	Social media (becoming the 'voice of' the trade)
	PR (trade focus)
	Direct mail
Business to consumer	Advertising
	Personal selling
	Sales promotions
	Direct marketing (post, telephone, email etc)
	Websites
	Social media
	Mobile
	PR (consumer focus)

Table 2.3 The communication mix in B2B and B2C markets

Consumer purchasing behaviour

Consumers make decisions about purchases after searching for information to support their decisions. But not every purchase involves the same amount of consideration or thought.

For example, purchase of fast-moving consumer goods (FMCG) is described as a **'routine response'** purchase. The consumer already has a great deal of knowledge and experience as they buy these goods regularly.

'Limited decision-making' or **'problem-solving'** occurs when the consumer is already familiar with the type of product they are looking to buy, even if they are unfamiliar with the brands available.

A consumer uses **'extensive decision-making'** or **'problem-solving'** when buying something for the first time. This might be a car, a mortgage or applying to a particular university.

Finally, consumers are described as **'impulse buying'** when they buy something they hadn't intended to. Their decision might have been triggered by an interesting display, or their purchase might be some sort of novelty product.

Marketers need to think about these different types of consumer behaviour in relation to the nature of product or service they offer.

Business-to-business purchasing behaviour

When shaping marketing activity and approaches in the B2B arena marketers need to consider the following types of purchase behaviour.

Straight re-buy – This is a repeat purchase of an existing product or service that has performed satisfactorily in the past. Customers don't need any new information. The existing supplier is usually difficult to displace as they have gained the buyer's trust and it easier for the buyer to maintain the status quo than to find a new supplier.

Modified re-buy – The buyer may be dissatisfied with the existing product or supplier and has to reconsider the buying decision. This usually means that the incumbent supplier loses the business to a competitor, usually as a result of incompetence or neglect.

New task buying – In this situation, there is no previous history. The buyer is looking for a product or service that he or she has not sourced before, and therefore all potential suppliers have the same chance of winning the business.

HOW MARKETS ARE SEGMENTED

Once organisations have decided which markets to operate in and which products or services to offer to those markets, they then have to work out how to compete in their chosen markets. Segmentation plays a vital role in their decision-making.

Kotler *et al* (1997) define **market segmentation** as:

"Dividing a market up into distinct groups of buyers with different needs, characteristics or behaviours, who might require separate products or marketing mixes."

Segmentation can be beneficial to organisations for a number of reasons. It allows them to:

- **Meet customers' needs more precisely**. Segmentation should increase benefits to customers by providing a closer match with their needs. An organisation can gain deeper market and customer knowledge on individual segments, allowing it to tailor its offerings.
- **Increase profits.** By grouping customers together based on their needs, organisations can obtain the best price for their products and services.
- **Gain segment leadership.** Most organisations are concerned with creating a specific competitive position and the leader's position confers benefits in the form of higher profits and return on investment (ROI). Focusing on a specific segment can also avoid competition with larger players.
- **Retain customers.** By providing specific products and services focused on specific needs, an organisation is more likely to generate loyalty among its customers.
- **Focus marketing communications.** Segmentation enables a firm to identify those most likely to buy from it, thus avoiding unnecessary communication and promotional effort.

Once the organisation has identified prospective segments, it has to evaluate them and decide which ones it will serve or target.

Kotler *et al* (1997) define **targeting** as:

"The process of evaluating each market segment's attractiveness and selecting one or more segments to enter."

Targeting involves evaluating market opportunities against their fit with the organisation. Are they aligned with the organisation's competencies and assets and is there a synergy with a particular market segment?

Once an organisation has selected its target markets it has to decide the position from which it will compete.

Kotler *et al* (1997) define **positioning** as:

"Arranging for a product to occupy a clear, distinctive and desirable place relative to competing products in the minds of target consumers. Formulating competitive positioning for a product and a detailed marketing mix."

In summary, **'segmentation, targeting and positioning'** (often known by the acronym STP) encompasses all the decisions organisations make in order to develop a specific competitive position:

- How do we define the market?
- How is the market segmented into different customer groups?
- How attractive are the different market segments?
- How strong a competitive position could we take based on our current and potential strengths?

When evaluating the attractiveness of a segment, marketers need to consider whether it is:

- Homogeneous – Do customers have similar needs?
- Measurable – Is data available to measure the segment?
- Substantial – Is the segment big enough in terms of sales and profitability to be worth targeting?.
- Accessible – Is the segment reachable through communications and distribution channels?
- Actionable – Can the company put a marketing mix together that targets the specific group?

Methods of segmenting consumer markets
These include:

Geographic segmentation – By county, region, or country.

Demographic segmentation – By factors such as age, gender, income, education, or family life-cycle stage.

Geodemographic segmentation – A combination of geographic and demographic segmentation methods.

Psychographic segmentation – By lifestyles or personality.

Behavioural segmentation – By factors such as customer attitudes towards the product, how frequently they buy it, what benefits they are seeking from it, and whether they are new or existing buyers or users.

Methods of segmenting B2B markets
Like marketers in other sectors, business-to-business marketers can use marketing research to identify potential customers, find out where

they are and estimate their purchase potential. But while they can segment their market using similar 'attractiveness' criteria, methods of segmenting the B2B market are different from in other markets.

Let's look at some examples.

Industry type – Most information about industrial customers is based on the Standard Industrial Classifications (SIC) system. This categorises all industrial, commercial, financial and service organisations by various economic characteristics. The kind of information available about industrial markets, for example, includes: value of shipments, number of establishments, number of employees, export and import data, industry growth rate and major producing regions.

The SIC system allows B2B marketers to divide industrial organisations into market segments based mainly on the type of product they manufacture or handle. Once they've identified target segments the marketers can identify and locate potential customers in those segments using the internet or business directories such as Kompass.

In the United States, the equivalent of the SIC system is the North American Industry Classification System (NAICS). There is also an International Standard Industry Classification (ISIC) system, which was introduced by the United Nations Statistics Division and covers all economic activities.

Benefit sought – In industrial marketing, it may be more beneficial to segment markets by benefit sought, rather than by customer characteristics. If a B2B marketer can gain a good insight into his customer's needs and understand how the product is going to be used, he is more likely to identify segmentation opportunities. For example a precious metal supplier could segment his market into those customers needing purity and those customers requiring strength.

Purchase potential – To estimate the purchase potential of B2B customers, the marketer has to find a relationship between the quantity purchased and a variable available from the SIC data, such as value of shipments or revenue. If the marketer knows that on average, the products he supplies are a known percentage of the buying organisation's costs, then he can calculate an average potential.

Other bases for segmenting business-to-business markets include:

Company demographics – For example, when was it established, where is it based, how many employees does it have, what is its turnover?

Purchasing approach – For example, is buying done centrally or is it decentralised, what are the buying criteria, what are the buying policies?

Situational factors – For example, the size or frequency of the order, the urgency of the purchase etc.

Operating variables – For example, the way the products or services are used by the customer.

Personal characteristics – The individual characteristics of the buyers within firms do have an impact on purchase behaviour. However formal the buying structure, individuals' personalities affect the way relationships develop, the ease with which a marketer can get to see a customer, and the ease with which they can sustain the relationship with the organisation should the individuals move to another company.

QUICK QUIZ – CHECK YOUR KNOWLEDGE

1. An understanding of customer buying behaviour is important to marketers. Which of the following best describes its value to an organisation?
   a. It ensures better cross-functional working.
   b. It bridges the gap between the organisation and its stakeholders.
   c. It helps the organisation to design better marketing programmes.
   d. It enables identification of market trends and competitiveness.

2. Organisational buying behaviour differs from consumer buying behaviour. Understanding these differences helps to shape which element of the marketing mix?
   a. Product.
   b. Price.
   c. Promotion.
   d. Place.

3. You work as a marketing assistant in a business-to-consumer organisation. Which of the following factors influence your customers' buying decisions?
   a. Organisational, environmental, individual and group.
   b. Social, personality, motivation and cultural.
   c. Cultural, environmental, individual and organisational.
   d. Cultural, organisational, group and motivation.

4. You work for an organisation that supplies jewellery direct to customers through its website and also to jewellery shops, which re-sell the products to their customers. Your manager has asked you to explain to other staff the key differences between consumer and organisational buying behaviour. Which of the following will you include on your list?

> **(1)** Nature of the product.
> **(2)** Lead time to purchase.
> **(3)** People involved.
> **(4)** Rationality.
> **(5)** Information requirements.

> **a.** All of the above.
> **b.** 1, 2 and 3 only.
> **c.** 1, 4 and 5 only.
> **d.** 2, 4 and 5 only.

(Answers: 1:c, 2:c, 3:b, 4:a)

3.

INFLUENCES ON MARKETING PLANNING

OUTLINE

This chapter gives an overview of the key influences on marketing planning from an organisation's macro, micro and internal environments. At the end of this chapter you will be able to:

- Identify key factors in the macro environment.
- Identify key factors in the micro environment.
- Identify key components of the internal environment.
- Explain the impact of macro, micro and internal factors on the marketing planning process.

DEFINITIONS

Competencies – An organisation's core competencies are the functional capabilities it uses to achieve its mission or strategic goals.

Corporate governance – The processes, systems and principles by which an organisation operates.

Corporate social responsibility (CSR) – The process by which an organisation minimises its negative impact and maximises its positive impact on society (as far as it is possible to do so).

Ethics – A set of principles that take account of the moral aspects of decisions.

Macro environment – The external factors that affect companies' planning and performance, and that are beyond its control (PESTELE factors).

Micro environment – The immediate context of a company's operations, including its suppliers, customers and competitors.

Resources – The portfolio of assets owned or managed by an organisation.

Stakeholder – An individual or group that affects or is affected by the organisation and its operations.

KEY FACTORS IN THE MACRO ENVIRONMENT

A useful model for examining the macro environment of a company is PESTELE analysis. PESTELE stands for political, economic, sociological, technological, environmental (or ecological), legal and ethical. These are all factors that make up the macro environment of an organisation and have an impact on the way it operates. This external analysis provides a picture of the opportunities available to the organisation, and the potential threats to it. Each of these seven areas comprises sub-factors, which affect the way the organisation operates at the highest level and the way it approaches all aspects of its marketing and selling.

Let's look at the type of factors that fall into each category.

Factors	Sub-factors
Political	Political and government stability Political orientation Taxation policies Pressure groups Trade Union strength
Economic	Business cycles Inflation rates Unemployment levels GNP trends Patterns of ownership
Sociological	Demographics Lifestyles Social issues Education levels Attitudes
Technological	Developments in technology Government investment in technology Product lifecycles
Environmental (or Ecological)	Green issues and climate change Waste
Legal	Competition law Employment law Foreign trade regulation Environmental protection legislation Consumer protection legislation
Ethical	Consumerism Corporate social responsibility

Table 3.1 Factors to consider in the macro environment

There are other frameworks that are used in similar ways to analyse the external environment. The table below shows how each of these link together. As you will see, PESTELE is the most comprehensive.

SLEPT	PEST	PESTELE	LEPEST
Sociological	Political (and legal)	Political	Legal
Legal	Economic	Economic	Economic
Economic	Sociological	Sociological	Political
Political	Technological	Technological	Ecological
Technological		Ecological	Sociological
		Legal	Technological
		Ethical	

Table 3.2 Frameworks for analysing the external environment

ACTIVITY 5

Your manager has asked you for a briefing paper that explains to staff in other departments the following elements of the macro environment, with an example factor from each:

- Sociological
- Legal
- Economic
- Technological

47

Ethics and social responsibility

Ethics are moral philosophies that define right and wrong behaviour – in marketing as elsewhere. Social responsibility is about minimising an organisation's negative impact and maximising its positive impact on society (as far as it is possible to do so within the constraints of the organisational model). These days companies that don't actively manage their social impact risk alienating key stakeholder groups, and this applies to marketers as much as (if not more than) anyone in the organisation.

CASE STUDY

To see examples of corporate social responsibility in practice look at www.j-sainsbury.co.uk/ and follow the link marked 'Responsibility'; and www.heinekencorp.com and follow the link marked 'Sustainability'.

Being seen to act unethically can seriously damage a company's reputation. While most companies operate within the law, some practices, while legal, are perceived as unethical. Most people regard as unacceptable the advertising of alcoholic drinks in a manner designed to appeal to youngsters, for example. There is also strong social opposition to tobacco advertising.

Marketers are expected to structure their campaigns and frame their messages responsibly, but they must also conduct their activities ethically. Contravening laws banning advertising to children or restricting the use of children in advertising would be unacceptable, for example.

CASE STUDY

The Chartered Institute of Marketing carried out a study in April 2014 entitled 'Keep Social Honest'. This was a response to the fact that social media and online reviews are now shaping customers' perceptions of brands. The results of the research suggest that companies should put in place ten rules to 'Keep Social Honest'.

1. Define and capture the right policies for your organisation.
2. Appoint and empower a champion and ambassadors.
3. Embed social media policies internally.
4. Share your social media position publicly (and proudly).
5. Make compliance with social media policies a professional development priority.
6. Involve your employees in social media, but put signposts in place.
7. Commit agency partners to shared 'good behaviours'.
8. Take an active role in the debate.
9. Revisit your policies and standards regularly.
10. Commit to abolishing 'no go' practices.

Developments in social media highlight the dynamic nature of marketing, but also demonstrate the reputational threats that need to be managed, as well as the opportunities to engage with customers, that such developments pose.

ACTIVITY 6

Your manager has asked you to prepare four slides for her to use in a short presentation to the board about the difference between ethics and social responsibility. Using PowerPoint, or a similar software package, produce the slides for the presentation.

KEY FACTORS IN THE MICRO ENVIRONMENT

Customers – To develop long-term relationships with customers, companies need to deliver consistent customer satisfaction and create real value for them. Earlier (in Chapter 1.2) we explored the concept of what customers perceive as value. It includes value for money, value through information, value through convenience, value through 'association' with the brand, and 'added value' – that is, something that is offered but does not appear to be charged for.

Competitors – Many companies express their marketing objectives in terms of securing a specified share of the market they operate in. In a commercial environment they will almost always have to contend with competitors. Even charities, despite their not-for-profit ethos, compete with each other for donor funds.

Companies operate in different markets, and understanding the state of competition in any given market helps the marketer make decisions.

If you don't monitor your competitors, you won't notice them wooing your customers, out-manoeuvring you with new products or services, undercutting you with sustainable price discounts, or out-flanking you by entering new markets.

In the next chapter we will explore some sources and types of information that are useful in monitoring aspects of the micro environment. The type of information you need to consider when analysing competitor behaviour, for example, include financial data and information about their resources, structure, plans, marketing activities (including marketing mix activity) and market share.

In summary, successful market-oriented companies find out what customers need, create value for those customers, operate efficiently and effectively, and find some means of achieving an advantage over their competitors for those customers. If you don't know your competitors, you won't be able to create competitive advantage.

ACTIVITY 7
List five sources of information you could use to monitor the competitive environment in your own industry.

Intermediaries – The relationship between an organisation and the members of its distribution channels (such as wholesalers and retailers) is also a significant factor in customer satisfaction. Because these intermediaries may also act for competitors, the organisation will have a vested interest in helping them to promote their products and in providing stock when they need it.

Suppliers – The relationship between an organisation and its suppliers is important if it is to maintain the supply of products and services to meet its customers' needs. A good relationship will help secure quality materials and components, delivered when you need them. However, if suppliers are dissatisfied they may start to supply competitors and reduce the level of service you have previously enjoyed.

From the above you will see that relationships with a wide range of stakeholders are very important.

Let's look at a sports club as an example. Like all businesses, sports clubs now understand the importance of communicating with their stakeholders, and developing marketing programmes and events to satisfy their needs. The stakeholders of a football club, for example, include:

- Supporters, customers and other 'users'.
- The local community – from which the club will draw many of these supporters, as well as potential employees. Also current employees and residents who live near the ground and may be affected by the arrival and departure of supporters.
- Police and other emergency services.
- Consumer and pressure groups.
- The media – local, national and international.
- Suppliers.
- Industry regulators and professional bodies.
- Sports bodies.
- Financial bodies and shareholders.
- Government bodies.

ACTIVITY 8

List three key stakeholders of your organisation and make notes on the impact they have on the organisation and how marketing is used to communicate with them.

KEY COMPONENTS OF THE INTERNAL ENVIRONMENT

An organisation's internal environment is made up of its core competences and resources, its corporate goals and objectives and issues such as corporate governance and risk management. It has to perform a delicate balancing act to meet its corporate objectives within the constraints that it works within. Let's look at each element in turn.

Resources and core competencies – Organisations have different levels of resources available to them. A small business has to limit its activity – including its marketing activity – according to the resources at its disposal. A much larger firm may have a high level of resources, but will also have larger goals to meet and competitors who also have high levels of resources.

The SWOT analysis (Strengths, Weaknesses, Opportunities, Threats) looks at the internal strengths and weaknesses of the organisation (its internal environment) and then examines where the organisation can use the identified strengths to take advantage of opportunities in the macro and micro environment. This analysis is useful in helping to shape the objectives and the strategy in the marketing plan.

Taking this a stage further, an organisation's resources and core competencies can be the source of sustainable competitive advantage. For example, a strong brand is a 'resource' that can enable a company to compete in one part of the market and gain a competitive edge.

Rothaermel (2012) says that if a resource is valuable (to customers), rare (so very few in a marketplace have it) and costly to imitate (so it is difficult for a competitor to achieve quickly), and the organisation is structured in such a way that the 'value' of the resource can be captured and used to advantage, then the competitive advantage can be termed 'sustainable'. An example of this might be Apple's reputation for brand design and innovation and the many patent challenges it has made (and won) against its competitor Samsung.

An organisation's resources and core competencies are its biggest asset. They are its functional capabilities, which it uses continuously to achieve its strategic goals.

Corporate goals and objectives – These provide the foundation for marketing's objectives. For example, if the organisation is focused on profitability, then marketing is unlikely to be looking to sell a high volume of products at a low price. Conversely, if the organisation is looking to increase its market share, then marketing may set its objectives around gaining a high share of the market by undercutting competitors' prices.

Corporate governance – These are the processes, systems and principles by which an organisation operates. It provides guidelines about how the organisation should be managing and controlling its activities, and it should ensure that everything runs in such a way that goals are achieved and all stakeholders satisfied.

Risk management – This is the process that identifies, analyses, controls, minimises or eliminates unacceptable risks to the business. Organisations can't set objectives without considering the risks associated with them.

3.4

THE IMPACT OF THESE FACTORS ON MARKETING PLANNING

Earlier in the module (Chapter 1.4) we looked at the marketing planning process. Let's now look at how changes in the environment can affect the organisation at each stage of the marketing planning process.

Situational analysis – During this stage the organisation will carry out a marketing audit, part of which involves auditing the macro environment. This audit identifies potential threats and opportunities, which the organisation can choose to respond to, depending on its capabilities and resources (or strengths and weaknesses). It will also conduct a risk analysis, the results of which will also inform decisions about what it should or shouldn't do.

The mission statement, vision and objectives – An organisation's objectives, vision and mission statements are a necessary and essential part of communication between it and its stakeholders.

The vision statement sets out what it imagines or foresees as its future potential and prospects. The vision helps everyone in the organisation to appreciate what it stands for and motivates them to progress.

A mission statement generally translates the vision statement into 'what business we are in and where we want to get to'. It is the first step towards getting organisational commitment to the vision and embedding it into everyday activity.

Analysis of the organisation's macro, micro and internal environments will help the organisation to set **SMART objectives** about where it wants to be in the future. By examining trends in the analysis, the organisation can arrive at some conclusions about what the future may hold, and this guides it in setting objectives that are achievable in, and relevant to, its changing environment.

SMART stands for **S**pecific, **M**easurable, **A**chievable, **R**elevant and **T**ime-bound. So, for example, an organisational objective might be: 'To be the leading global supplier of healthy fruit drinks (**S**) for children by 2016 (**T**), with a market share of 15 per cent (**M**, **R**, **A**).'

Objectives generally fall into one of three categories:

- To maximise profit for the organisation.
- To maximise benefit for society as a whole or a specific section of society.
- To maximise benefit for customers.

To maximise profit for the organisation – commercial organisations. The restaurant chain Pizza Hut is under new ownership. In seeking to maximise profits it has closed some underperforming restaurants and reduced the number of special offers it gives to customers.

To maximise benefit for society as a whole, or a particular section of society – charities and voluntary organisations. The stated vision of the international charity Water Aid is a world where everyone has access to safe water and sanitation.

To maximise benefits for members – mutual organisations and co-operatives. CIM is this sort of organisation and its purpose is 'To develop the profession and those who work within it for the benefit of the economy and society.'

Strategy – This is how organisations achieve their objectives. Again, the changing environment will influence their choice of strategic options. For example, changes in demographic trends may change the profile of the working population. Growth in the service sector in the UK, for instance, has increased the number of older workers. This has opened up new target markets for some companies, extended existing markets for others, and closed markets for yet others.

Tactics/implementation – Understanding the environment will affect the marketing mix the organisation adopts and the way it implements the marketing plan. For example, relationships with financial stakeholder groups (banks, in effect) will have an effect on the resources available to implement the plan. Staff skills will affect the way the plan is carried out and action by pressure groups may influence promotional activity.

QUICK QUIZ – CHECK YOUR KNOWLEDGE
1. Which of the following best represents an organisation's external macro-environment?
   a. Social, legal, competitor, ecological and ethical factors.
   b. Social, technical, economic, ecological, ethical, political and legal factors.
   c. Competitors, customers, suppliers and intermediaries.
   d. Resources, competencies, corporate governance and goals.

2. Which of the following is most likely to be guided by the outcome of the marketing audit?

    (1) Setting of objectives.
    (2) Selection of strategy.
    (3) Staff skill development.
    (4) Research briefs.

    a. 1 and 2 only.
    b. All of the above.
    c. 2 and 4 only.
    d. 1, 2 and 3 only.

3. Which of the following best represents an organisation's external micro environment?
    a. Social, legal, competitor, ecological and ethical factors.
    b. Social, technical, economic, ecological, ethical, political and legal factors.
    c. Customers, competitors, stakeholders, suppliers and distributors.
    d. Resources, competencies, corporate governance and goals.

4. Which of the following models would you choose to analyse your marketing environment?
    a. APIC
    b. PESTELE
    c. SMART
    d. SOSTAC®

(Answers: 1:b, 2:a, 3:c, 4:b)

55

4.

GATHERING MARKETING INFORMATION

OUTLINE

This chapter gives an overview of the different types of information that are useful to marketers in generating insights to shape marketing activity. At the end of this chapter you will be able to:

- Describe key information types.
- Explain the techniques that can be used to collect primary data.
- Identify relevant sources of secondary information on markets, customers and competitors.
- Demonstrate how to manage and interpret information in order to create insights.

DEFINITIONS

Category management – A retailing concept in which the range of products sold is broken down into discrete groups of similar or related products, known as 'product categories'.

Environmental scanning – Monitoring an organisation's external environment in order to spot or anticipate emerging issues. This provides an early warning of changing external conditions.

Marketing information system (MKIS) – Practices and procedures to gather, sort, store, analyse and distribute marketing information to aid the marketing decision-making process.

Market insight – Breakthrough understanding of the market that directs you towards new and improved ways to serve customers.

Primary research – Carried out specifically to answer the questions raised in a market research brief.

Qualitative data – Information that can't be measured or expressed in numeric terms. Explores feelings and opinions.

Quantitative data – Information that can be measured in numeric terms and analysed statistically.

Secondary data – Data sourced from that which already exists and has been gathered for another purpose or objective.

KEY INFORMATION TYPES

Primary research – Also known as field research, is carried out specifically to answer the questions raised in a market research brief. It includes surveys (postal, face to face, telephone and internet), depth interviews, focus groups, 'projective' techniques, experiments and observations.

Secondary research – Also referred to as desk research, involves investigating data that already exists. It may take the form of internal records, or reports that have been collated for another purpose. It is usually done before primary research, and is much cheaper and typically less time consuming. However, because this data hasn't been gathered for the specific purpose marketers are now considering, it has limitations.

Information sourced through either secondary or primary techniques can be either qualitative or quantitative. And it may be gathered from internal or external sources.

Qualitative information can't be measured or expressed in numeric terms. It is useful to the marketer as it often explores people's feelings and opinions.

Quantitative information *can* be measured and expressed in numeric terms – for example, the percentage market share held, the number of customers buying a product in a certain month, or the number of sales calls made in a week.

4.2

TECHNIQUES FOR COLLECTING PRIMARY DATA

Primary research techniques include the following.

Self-completion surveys – These are completed by the targeted individual respondent, to whom they are sent via email or post. Increasingly there are self-completion questionnaires on websites, but because the respondents answering the questions are self-selecting this limits the value of the response. This type of questionnaire is cheapest to administer as it doesn't require an interviewer, either on the phone or face to face. However, it is also the least likely to be completed, and so has the lowest response rate. This means that the end result can be based on an unrepresentative sample. The most effective self-completion surveys are usually those that require 'tick box' answers.

Surveys via interview – These can be face to face or over the telephone, structured, semi-structured, or unstructured. Structured surveys are fully constrained by the requirements of the questionnaire, which is usually of a 'tick box' nature. Semi-structured surveys use a questionnaire that has a combination of tick box and open-ended questions, allowing a degree of probing. Unstructured interviews are used to elicit qualitative data, and the interviewer usually just has a list of topics to discuss.

Surveys by interview have a higher response rate than postal or email surveys, and face-to-face surveys generally have a slightly better response rate than telephone surveys. Telephone surveys are quicker and more economical, but again there is a danger that they are an unrepresentative sample, as individuals with ex-directory numbers those registered with the Telephone Preference Service can't be included.

Focus groups – These also produce valuable qualitative data, and are useful in that they provide the opportunity for an individual's comments to 'spark off' ideas and discussion from others in the group. The group is usually made up of eight to ten members, and the value of the data gathered depends on the selection of respondents and the competence of the group 'moderator', who needs to be carefully trained.

Observation – This technique is increasingly used in retail environments. It looks at shopping behaviour and is used to inform category management. Video cameras are often used, although 'headcounts' are still carried out by personal observers. This can be relatively expensive, but reports on shopping behaviour may be jointly commissioned, spreading the cost.

Mystery shopping – Mystery shopping programmes are usually run by external specialist agencies. They involve selecting 'customers' from a database who most closely match an organisation's current customer base. These researchers are asked to make a specific purchase or enquiry and report back in a structured way about their experience and how customer-facing employees dealt with them.

Experimentation – Test marketing is the most obvious form of experimentation, where, for example, a mini-launch of a new product may take place in a smaller, similar market to the intended one. This allows marketers to consider customers' responses to the product itself, and its promotion, without the risk and cost of a full launch. Simulations and laboratory tests are also forms of experimentation.

CASE STUDY

A good example of the way marketers use research to check out the market, its wants and needs, and its competitors, is the development and launch of Instagram. This started life as a fully developed location-based app called Burbn. Its developers carried out research before launching in a big way, and found that their product was perceived to be cluttered with features, and that they had been beaten to the market by Foursquare. They decided to de-clutter it down to just photos and then rebranded it as Instagram. Facebook purchased Instagram for $1bn in 2012. Research transformed early failure into spectacular success.

ACTIVITY 9

For an in-house marketing research training day with your team you have been asked to produce a handout that:

- Provides a list of clear examples of the different tools used to gather different types of marketing research.
- Describes the advantages and disadvantages of each example listed.

SOURCES OF SECONDARY DATA

Sources of secondary data on markets, customers and competitors include those in the table below.

Government sources	Governments produce statistics on many areas, including population censuses, family expenditure surveys, import/export statistics, production statistics and social surveys.
Commercial market research reports	Produced by organisations such as Mintel and Key Note, these industry reports are based on panel surveys and provide information on consumer activity and business-to-business markets.
Trade and industry sources	Trade and industry bodies publish directories and other industry statistics, plus member survey results.
Competitor data	Reports and Accounts are available on corporate websites, as well as evidence of marketing activity and plans.
Online information sources	Competitor websites, online databases.
Media sources	Quality business newspapers (such as the *Financial Times*) and specialised trade press (*The Grocer*, for example).
Social media feeds and blogs	Feeds from influential blogs can alert you to what's happening in the market, and tools such as 'mention' can send you an alert whenever you or a competitor is mentioned in social media.
Financial, geographic and demographic databases	Economic reviews, country reports and population databases.
Internal databases and records – from store audits or scanned data, for example	Data might include sales figures, call reports, CRM entries and financial reports.

Table 4.1 Sources of secondary data

4.4

MANAGING AND INTERPRETING INFORMATION TO GAIN INSIGHTS

The purpose of a **Marketing Information System (MKIS)** is to give the right information to the right people at the right time, in the most cost-effective and efficient manner possible.

The system will usually provide decision-makers with appropriate and useful insights to aid their decision-making, but it can also provide a wider range of people with more general information to keep them fully informed about the issues that affect them and their area of responsibility. Although the modern MKIS is usually computer based, it doesn't have to be.

The MKIS may comprise various sub-elements, such as:

- The internal reports system.
- The marketing intelligence system.
- The marketing research system.
- The analytical marketing system.

The internal reports system – This monitors and reports on areas such as orders, sales, stock levels, accounts receivable and accounts payable. These reports can highlight problem areas, enabling managers to react appropriately by making informed decisions (perhaps to reduce stock or extend credit to customers, for example).

The marketing intelligence system – This is likely to incorporate inputs derived from both formal and informal information-gathering activities. This usually requires marketers to be proactive and take advantage of the skills or situation of employees by encouraging them to collect useful intelligence when they read the trade press, visit trade exhibitions or meet customers or distributors. Web analytics can produce relevant and detailed insights into customers' online behaviour, giving the organisation in-depth information into what it needs to improve, what conversations are taking place on social media sites and 'sentiment' about the brand.

The marketing research system – This typically involves the systematic design, collection and analysis of data, plus the reporting and presentation of the findings. It may include various primary research activities, such as customer surveys or focus groups. This research can be done either in-house or by a specialist research agency.

The analytical marketing system – This is the element of the MKIS that uses statistical procedures and mathematical models to analyse data and produce insights that can inform marketing decisions and activity.

62

The value of the information provided to the users of an information system depends on its:

- Relevance.
- Completeness.
- Accuracy.
- Clarity.
- Timeliness.

Not only can a good information system give a company competitive edge by delivering accurate, timely information that allows it to respond quickly to opportunities and threats, but a healthy flow of information can also help team-working, communication and motivation.

You can share information in a variety of ways – written reports, email, web pages, disks or video.

Just like the finance information system, the human resources information system and other functional-area information systems, the Marketing Information System (MKIS) is a sub-system of the Management Information System (MIS).

A fully integrated MIS allows managers to make decisions based on a range of factors. This means marketing decisions can also take account of other issues (such as the availability of resources, stock levels or cash flow). Some elements of a complete MIS may involve some form of primary research activity too, but the MKIS is the main system used to gather data and information for marketing purposes.

The information from an information system should provide users with the following benefits.

Reduces uncertainty and risk – Information systems can provide information that helps to reduce uncertainty. In a marketing context this could mean helping to ensure that all the elements of the marketing mix are developed appropriately – for example, that prices are set at a level that maximises profit without reducing sales, and that new products and services are developed to satisfy changing customer needs. Such systems are often used when developing new products to help determine the risk of failure and provide guidance as to how to adjust plans to ensure the new product is successful.

Monitors performance against plans – Every organisation needs to know that its systems and processes are efficient and effective, and it can only know this if it monitors actual performance and results against the outcomes or targets it expected. The systems produce information that can help managers to evaluate the performance of individuals or departments and to ensure that corporate and marketing objectives are being achieved. They can also provide information on customer satisfaction.

Contributes to strategic processes – Organisations need to adapt to changing circumstances by developing appropriate and successful strategies. Marketers can use information about changes in the external environment to help their organisation differentiate itself from its competitors and to continue to meet the needs of existing and new markets. The process of continuously monitoring the external environment for such changes is referred to as environmental scanning.

ACTIVITY 10

To be valuable, the information generated by an information system must fulfil certain criteria.

List the five criteria that make information valuable and, with reference to a source of information that your own marketing department uses, comment briefly on how well it meets those criteria.

Forecasting for business decisions

Forecasting is an attempt to know the future. But of course we can't predict with any degree of accuracy what the future will bring. This puts marketers in a rather tricky, but pivotal, position: they are paid to predict, as accurately as possible, future sales, the success of projects and the return on investment in new products and services. Their organisations set great store by these forecasts as they base business decisions and plans on them.

Why do we need forecasting? After all, some entrepreneurs are proud of having ignored all rational advice and launched products and services based on gut feel. We hear about all the success stories, of course, but rarely the failures. Basing investment decisions on instinct alone is a high-risk strategy and isn't good business practice. If it's your own money, that's one thing, but if you are using shareholders' money (in the form of capital) or banks' money (in the form of loans) you need to adopt a more rational and professional approach.

Organisations employ marketing professionals directly or in agencies to investigate the future and provide forecasts, not guesses, based on data. Decision-makers use such forecasts to judge the viability of projects in order to ensure that they use the organisation's resources as effectively and efficiently as possible.

Decision-makers and accountants use marketing forecasts to help them decide where to invest the organisation's funds. The key questions they will want answers to are how much money a project needs and what the likely return on investment will be.

Quantitative forecasting answers questions such as the following. How many can we sell? How much for? What is the size of the current market? What is the potential market size?

Qualitative forecasting answers questions such as the following. What are people's attitudes towards a project or brand? Will people change their existing habits? How will their tastes evolve?

All these questions are concerned with the application of money to projects. To arrive at the answers, marketers need to gather as much data as possible to support a business case. This is the forecast. Once the forecast shows that there is indeed an opportunity, the decision-makers can prepare a budget for it.

QUICK QUIZ – CHECK YOUR KNOWLEDGE

1. You work for a global organisation and market consumer goods through your own branded range of retail outlets. Recently, sales have been falling even though marketing activity remains high. Your marketing manager has noticed from annual customer surveys that customer satisfaction appears to be falling. He thinks that this may be the result of falling service levels in the retail outlets. He has asked you to carry out some research to investigate this further. Which of the following would you select in order to gain insight into this topic to report back?
   a. Sales data analysis.
   b. In-depth interviews.
   c. Mystery shopping.
   d. Observation.

2. Which of the following questions might you use in quantitative research?
   a. In your opinion, why do most people buy XYZ brand?
   b. What makes you say that?
   c. How often do you buy ABC brand?
   d. Why do you think that?

3. The marketing manager has asked you for information to support a report she's writing about your marketplace. You only have two days to find the information and there is very little budget available. Which **one** of the following would be the most suitable for your research?
   a. Primary data.
   b. Secondary data.
   c. Sampling.
   d. Qualitative data.

4. Which of the following is a method of gathering qualitative data?
   a. Focus group.
   b. Time series.
   c. Extrapolation.
   d. Sales data analysis.

(Answers: 1:c, 2:c, 3:b, 4:a)

5.
THE MARKETING MIX

OUTLINE

In previous chapters we have examined the concept of marketing, the importance of customers, and the value in gathering and interpreting marketing information to support decisions such as what marketing and corporate objectives to develop. This chapter moves on to a further stage in the marketing planning process, the development of marketing tactics, using the marketing mix.

The marketing mix, or '4 Ps', is a framework that, in essence, helps the marketer to decide where, how and for what price they should be selling their products or services. When deciding on the appropriate marketing mix for any product or service, the marketer's objectives are to satisfy the needs of a target segment of customers and to deliver value to the organisation.

At the end of this chapter you will be able to:

- Describe the four key elements of the marketing mix (the '4Ps').
- Describe the three key elements in the extended marketing mix (the '7Ps').
- Explain the importance of developing a co-ordinated approach to the marketing mix.

DEFINITIONS

The marketing mix or '4Ps' (Product, Price, Promotion and Place) – The tactics that marketers use to meet the needs of key stakeholders.

The extended marketing mix or '7Ps' – People, Process and Physical Evidence are added to the marketing mix to take into account the unique nature of services and provide marketers with additional tactical options.

The co-ordinated mix – The elements of the 7P marketing mix designed and implemented to support and add value to each other.

Distribution – The 'Place' element of the marketing mix. Concerned with how the product or service reaches the end user based on the characteristics of the marketplace and the make-up of the product or service.

Media – The tools that can be used to deliver marketing messages, for example broadcast, digital, print and outdoor.

Message – A piece of communication that may contain a variety of signs, symbols and content that is designed to appeal to the audience and influence attitudes.

5.1

THE FOUR KEY ELEMENTS OF THE MARKETING MIX

The traditional marketing mix is made up of four main components, each of which has its own individual mix of activities.

Product – The product mix involves decisions about new product development, which products to continue or discontinue and product modifications to keep pace with changing customer needs and changes in the external environment.

Price – The price mix involves decisions on pricing policy, methods and tactics. It links the pricing of products to the desired positioning of the product in the mind of the consumer, and ensures the price suggests an appropriate quality image for the product or service.

Place – The place mix involves decisions about distribution, such as the costs of getting products to the consumer, and the options to do so. It covers issues like the selection of intermediaries and logistics such as storage and transport systems.

Promotion – The promotional mix involves decisions about which promotional tools are most appropriate for the target audience, what message is suitable, co-ordinating the tools in order to communicate a consistent message, and which media to use.

Let's consider each element of the 4P marketing mix in turn.

1. PRODUCT

Products can be classified into several categories for both consumer and business-to-business markets.

The main categories for consumer goods are the following.

Convenience goods – Sometimes referred to as commodities, these include milk, sugar, rice, potatoes and the kind of items that feature on a regular shopping list.

Shopping goods – More durable goods such as electrical appliances, furniture, car, etc. The consumer spends longer in the information search phase of buying decisions than they do for convenience goods.

Speciality goods – More exclusive items such as luxury cruises, designer clothes and jewellery. Prices are extremely high and purchase decisions are made after an extensive search process.

Business-to-business goods can also be classified, but the categories are very different.

Raw materials – Rubber, metal etc – things that are essential in the production of the final product.

MARKETING

Components – Items that are used in the production of the final product, but have already been through some process, usually carried out by a supplier.

Supplies – Things like cleaning materials, stationery and so on, which, although not involved in the production of the final product, are essential to the day-to-day running of the business.

Accessories – Again, not part of the final product, but essential for the running of the business. These include office equipment, furniture etc.

Installations – These include the capital goods that the company needs to make its final product, such as plant and machinery.

Marketers need to consider product classifications when putting together the marketing mix for the product, because they provide information about acceptable prices for each category and how best to promote them.

Organisations operating in not-for-profit (third sector) and public sectors have additional 'product' considerations. These may not be 'products' in the sense that we traditionally think of them – that is, as goods sold to a consumer or a business – but services, ideas or requests for donations or contributions.

The product, whatever category it falls into, is made up of a '**bundle of benefits**' that is offered as a package to the customer, and together these benefits contribute significantly to the value the customer attaches to the product.

There are three levels to this product 'bundle' or '**total product concept**'.

The **core product** – This is the core benefit that the product or service offers. The core benefit of a car, for example, is that it transports the user from A to B.

The **actual product** – This includes the features and capabilities of the product, along with the brand name, packaging, quality and design. In a car these features deliver benefits such as comfort, style and safety.

The **augmented product** – This adds further value through warranties and guarantees, customer service or technical support, and delivery and installation if appropriate. The purchase of a new car, for example, may include membership of a recovery service or a warranty.

Each customer will place a different emphasis on the benefits offered. Some of the benefits may be irrelevant to them – the recovery service is a prime example. One purchaser may be delighted by this benefit, whereas others may already be covered through their bank or their partner, so wouldn't derive much value from it.

Over time **actual** features can become **core** features, and **augmented** features become **actual** features, as customers' expectations grow. This means that companies have to introduce new features, usually in the **augmented** product, to distinguish it from competitors.

Branding

A brand can form part of the product's features and helps the customer identify its unique characteristics. A brand can be defined as a name, term, design, symbol or any other feature that fulfils this purpose. Branding is highly important in competitive markets, because it helps to differentiate one company's products from another's. Customers associate particular values and a certain level of quality with each brand.

Companies can use a successful brand name to help introduce new products to the market. However, in seeking to extend the product portfolio they need to guard against stretching the brand too far, because this can dilute its power.

Organisations have to protect their brands, which, as we noted earlier, are valuable resources for them. Trademarks are one way, but supporting consistent product quality and performance with a powerful message to existing and potential customers is even more effective.

Packaging

How to package a product is an important decision for the marketer, and links closely to an understanding of buyer behaviour. Packaging is said to fulfil four roles – **protection**, **promotion**, **provision of information** and **convenience**.

Protection – The marketer needs to think about the nature of the product and how best to protect it through its channel to market. For example, food items need to be protected from bacteria and, increasingly, be tamper proof. A music CD needs to be protected from becoming scratched or damaged, so that it will play and provide the benefit the customer is seeking.

Promotion – It is very important that the packaging is consistent with the brand and the image portrayed in all other forms of communication. This is covered further in the Promotion section of this chapter below.

Provision of information – Packaging legislation dictates what must be on a package or its label. For example, food stuffs need to be labelled with a name, 'best before' or 'use by' date, quantity, ingredients and, increasingly, things like salt, fat and sugar content (to name but a few). Information may also become part of the product, either in the sense of describing to customers how to use it, or telling 'stories' about its provenance.

Convenience – The main characteristic here links to pricing. For example, reusable packs may allow marketers to offer cheaper prices for refills; smaller packs may make products more affordable; and multipacks may be offered with cost savings. The size of the package can also relate to buyer behaviour. For example, a large family may buy a large pack of washing powder, whereas someone about to go on holiday may buy a small convenience pack.

Considering the roles that packaging performs serves to re-emphasise the links between the different elements of the marketing mix. For example:

- Smaller packs and lower **prices**.
- Packaging and **promotion** of the brand.
- Multipacks for sub-division by wholesalers (**place**).

2. PRICE

Price is an important element of the marketing mix. It helps to position the product or service in a competitive market place, it reflects the value the organisation attributes to the product and brand, and it can be adapted to changing external environmental factors.

An organisation has to take many factors into account when deciding on its pricing policy. These include the size of the organisation and its objectives, the level of demand for the product, the amount of competition in the marketplace and how much it costs to produce and distribute the product. We list below some of the factors that affect pricing decisions.

Company and marketing objectives – Everything the marketing department does should reflect corporate objectives, and, in turn, marketing objectives. An organisation that is looking to grow market share may need to reduce prices in the short term, whereas an organisation that is looking to improve profitability would not achieve its objective by following the same pricing strategy. An organisation looking to improve profitability may increase the price slightly, or focus internally on operating costs.

Company resources – Decisions about prices have to take account of the level of resources available to the organisation over a period of time. For example, price competition is a familiar sight in retailing, and supermarkets have waged 'price wars' since the late 1990s. In order to be able to flex their prices they have had to drive down the costs of suppliers and the costs within their own operations. The main danger of price wars is that organisations can't sustain the downward spiral of prices, as competitors continue to find new ways of producing more efficiently and cheaply. This risk is particularly acute in undifferentiated markets, such as petrol, where the only difference between competing products is price. If one major player in the market is forced to raise prices, rivals may continue to hold theirs down to gain additional volume.

CASE STUDY

The long-running supermarket 'price wars' are the subject of regular media discussion. These wars raged more fiercely still during and immediately after the global financial crisis that reached the UK in 2007. Disposable incomes shrank and competition spread from the 'Big Four' to include European discounters Aldi and Lidl too.

The discounters are now generating double-digit growth percentages, while profits at the likes of Tesco and Morrisons are declining. The discounters are proving to be a very real threat in the supermarket sector.

But how should the 'Big Four' respond? What is the best way to recoup lost market share? Currently, one of the Big Four is looking to use marketing communications to undermine the perceived quality of the discounters, while a second is set to compete directly on price.

Product costs – Price and cost are different. **Price** is how much a company sells its product for; **cost** is how much it costs to make and get to market. Although costs are not the only factor in setting prices, they are a significant factor in the pricing decision, and the marketer has to consider the cost structure of the firm when setting prices.

Cutting costs in order to reduce prices can lead to a reduction in the quality of services offered, or a lack of innovation or research and development, because operations become internally focused on reducing overheads and costs. Therefore, survivors of a price war may be leaner, but they are not necessarily fitter, and they may well have lost sight of customer needs. Customer loyalty is difficult to sustain during price wars, as buyers are encouraged to evaluate alternatives on price alone and switch between brands offering the best deal.

Market demand – This is extremely important to the marketer. There is a point where the market will no longer accept the price set for a product or service. The marketer needs to think about how they will cope with supply if the price is too low, and what will happen to the volume of sales if the price is too high.

We talk about the '**price elasticity**' of demand. When the demand for a product doesn't change much when the price is adjusted, we refer to the product as being 'price inelastic'. When price changes result in relatively large shifts in demand, then the product is 'price elastic'.

When looking at demand, you have to consider the buyer's perception of the value offered by the product or service. The whole of the co-ordinated marketing mix, combined with the customer's expectations and previous experience of the product, will affect this perception.

Competition/market structure – The level of competition varies between different markets. In markets where there are few competitors, the largest companies tend to take a lead that the other companies have to follow. Where there are many companies offering very similar products, price competition is typically much more acute.

When faced with a high level of competition, companies often try to differentiate their product through quality, communications, customer service or special product features, so that they are not pushed out of business by their 'price-setting' competitors.

Companies also have to think about how easy it is for new competitors to enter the market, as this may also affect their pricing decisions.

Pricing policies

'Pricing policy' is the term used to describe the overall approach that an organisation takes to pricing. It covers things like how it prices against competitors (just above or just below the main competitor, for example), and whether or not it will use price promotions (two-for-one offers, etc). When looking to set a price, the marketer has to consider a number of factors:

- Company objectives.
- The desired positioning of the product in the minds of the target segment(s).
- What price the target market will bear.
- Market demand, as well as the relationships between cost, volume and profit.
- The competitive situation, and what competitors charge.
- Product life-cycle stage.
- Overall marketing mix.

When a company wants to launch a new product it may choose between two main pricing strategies. **Market penetration** involves setting a low price to gain a high volume of sales, whereas **market skimming** involves setting the price at a higher level and positioning the product to 'skim' the top of the market.

Pricing tactics or methods

A marketer has a number of different pricing methods to choose from to help the organisation compete. For example, it is a rare organisation that offers only one product, so marketers can adjust prices across the product portfolio to maximise profits. Pricing tactics include:

- **Product line pricing** – Products across a product line have their prices 'stepped' according to the difference in their cost to produce, their benefits or features, different market segments and the way competitors price their equivalents. For example, different shampoos produced by the same organisation are likely to be priced differently, particularly where organisations adopt a multi-brand approach.
- **Optional product pricing** – This is a tactic that involves selling a basic product with a range of optional extras. Cars, for example, are offered as a basic model, or with the options of air-conditioning, tinted windows, alloy wheels, DAB radio etc.
- **Product bundle pricing** – Products are bundled together and sold cheaper than when sold separately. Multipacks of crisps are an example: families can gain small cost savings when buying packs containing six or twelve individual packs.

Pricing strategies, whether for a product or portfolio of products, include:

- **Cost-plus pricing** – A simple pricing method that involves calculating the costs involved in producing a product (including the research and development costs), then adding a fixed percentage profit to these costs to arrive at a price. This method does not suit the marketer, as it takes no account of what the market considers value for money. It is used widely in contracting.
- **Demand-based pricing** – The most marketing-orientated way of setting a price. Marketers use primary research to find out what potential customers are prepared to pay for a product.
- **Competitor parity** – Where prices are matched to the competition. This means that products must be differentiated from the competition in some way in order to give the product a competitive advantage.
- **Psychological pricing** – Involves setting prices at set 'price points', such as $399.95, or £19.99, in the hope that customers feel they are paying significantly less than if the price was $400 or £20.

3. PLACE

When they develop a distribution network companies can choose from a range of possible channels to market, including agents, distributors, wholesalers, retailers and going direct to the consumer. The internet facilitates a direct route to market, but, like all channels, it has disadvantages as well as advantages. We explore each of these channels below.

Agents – These can be manufacturers' agents, selling agents, brokers, fundraising agents or commission merchants. They don't usually take title or ownership of the products or services, but receive a commission for facilitating the exchange between a seller and a buyer.

Distributors – These generally *do* take ownership of the goods, on which they charge a mark-up or handling fee or the manufacturer's recommended price (which includes a margin). However, not all distributors deal with end users.

Wholesalers – These perform a wide range of functions for the manufacturer at one end of the chain and for the retailer at the other end. These functions, or services, usually more than compensate for the proportion of profit the wholesalers take from the manufacturer.

Functions provided by wholesalers for the manufacturer include:

- Promotional activity.
- Warehousing, storage and 'breaking up' of stock.
- Some of the transport arrangements.
- Inventory control.
- Feedback, particularly about competitor activity and prices.
- Credit control.

For the retailer they include:

- Passing on information.
- Providing a 'one-stop' shopping environment for the smaller retailer.
- Making smaller purchases available.
- Fast delivery/collection facilities.

Retailers – These include the corner shop, the high street shop, supermarkets and convenience stores. Retailers deal almost exclusively with end-consumers of goods, or customers purchasing consumer goods for their family and friends, rather than with businesses.

Direct routes – These involve the manufacturer or producer dealing direct with either the end-consumer or the business buying their product. Routes include direct mail-order (often with a catalogue), telesales, the internet or a company's own sales force. Being able to fulfil orders efficiently is key in this method of distribution, and this can be run in-house or outsourced.

Factors affecting place or channel decisions

The factors that can affect the choice of distribution channel and/or method of transportation can include the following.

Where the market is and the likely sales volume – Is your market spread over a large geographical area? Is it well contained in one region of a country? Also, what volume of sales/revenue are you likely to make in any one area? These issues will have a major impact on whether you outsource transportation or use your own fleet of vehicles.

Product characteristics – Fragile and perishable products need shorter channels so as to minimise spoilage. When transporting overseas, perishable products may warrant the higher cost of air freight, because, balanced against the cost of spoilage on a longer sea journey, it may actually work out cheaper.

Competitor activity – Can you achieve a competitive advantage by choosing a different route to market from the competition? Consider the impact that digital distribution has had on the market place.

Cost – The organisation's resources will obviously influence the choice of distribution channel, but the example used in 'product characteristics' above is also relevant.

Reliability – How much control do you need over the channel? If you need tight control to protect the brand for example, then a shorter chain will be more manageable.

Security issues – High-value items will often need to be distributed exclusively through specialist outlets, or via mail order.

Level of customer service required – Does the customer need fast delivery? If so, you might need to hire a courier. How complex is the buying decision? With complex products or services, consumer markets tend to rely on retailers, who offer face-to-face contact and can explain products or services properly. In business-to-business markets companies tend to use their own sales force to pass on expert knowledge.

Legal issues – Legislation such as the Competition Act, Fair Trading Act, Trade Descriptions Act, Data Protection Act and Consumer Protection Act has an impact on channel decisions. For example, the Data Protection Act affects companies that hold personal customer data for direct distribution. In the past, some wholesalers and dealers refused to implement anti-competitive practices that manufacturers tried to impose on them, and as a result were blacklisted by the manufacturers. This is now illegal under the Competition Act.

4. PROMOTION

The promotional mix is made up of advertising, public relations, sales promotion, direct marketing and personal selling. These five tools within the promotional, or communications, mix include many different channels and media, some of which are covered below.

Advertising – This includes media such as television, radio, print, cinema, outdoor and internet advertising. These media and the messages delivered can be used, to varying degrees, to **D**ifferentiate a product or service, **R**emind customers of the benefits of a product or service, **I**nform or educate potential customers who may be going through the information search phase of the buying process, and **P**ersuade them to think, feel or act in a certain way.

It is useful to remember the mnemonic **DRIP**, as it sets out the different tasks that all promotions can be used to achieve.

More and more adverts are now directing audiences to websites to obtain even more information through interactive components such as red button integration, QR codes, even apps like Shazam. Advertising can be used not only to raise awareness of a product around its launch, but also to keep reminding the public of its existence during the year. It can also help to balance the effects of negative publicity.

CASE STUDY

Shazam began life as an application to identify, or 'tag', a song that was playing in the real world. It still does this, but Shazam has recently developed another use of the app in order to grow its business. It is now partnering with TV media companies and agencies to add interactivity to broadcast, predominantly TV, adverts.

The idea is that when the user tags the audio content of an advert they are taken to more engaging, interactive content via their 'second screen' – either a tablet or smartphone. Brands such as Sony, Pepsi, Cadbury, Barclaycard and Microsoft have all used Shazam and have significantly increased consumer engagement with their brand and online content as a result.

Public relations – Companies can attract an enormous amount of publicity – and not all of it positive. PR, used properly, can help to develop links with the press and other key stakeholders that may help to minimise or mitigate any negative coverage.

We can define public relations (PR) as 'a planned and sustained effort to establish and maintain goodwill between an organisation and its publics'. Regional events, charity associations and community relations are examples of activities companies can organise to promote a positive image to a target audience. Companies can also use PR to reinforce advertising in creating awareness.

Ultimately, PR is a tool for building a positive perception of the organisation, brand and/or product in the minds of its different stakeholders.

Sales promotion – This involves offering inducements or incentives to customers. A tourist attraction, for example, might offer reduced-price tickets to groups because of the volume of sales. It might make similar offers at quieter times (term time, for example) to incentivise other groups to visit.

Generally, a sales promotion is designed to increase sales in the short term, and is not aimed at achieving long-term customer loyalty. However, some companies have developed loyalty over time through a more strategic use of sales promotions. Reward schemes for existing customers such as Tesco Clubcard, Nectar or even O_2 Priority Moments are essentially sales promotions, but designed to add value over the longer term.

Organisations use these loyalty cards or reward systems to build databases of information about their customers and their preferences, in order to target promotions more effectively. They gather information in a number of other ways too, including post-purchase customer satisfaction surveys and records of individual customer purchases. For example, car dealerships may store information about the date and nature of a customer's most recent purchase, their age, social grouping and family status, so that they can target those customers most likely to buy when they launch a new model, or most likely to take a new vehicle when a lease is about to expire.

It is increasingly important for traditional 'bricks and mortar' retailers to keep in touch with their customers and their changing requirements, because customers have growing opportunities to purchase elsewhere. Internet shopping is increasingly popular as consumers become more confident about security and more willing to use technology. Many Christmas shoppers shop online to avoid the crowds or engage in 'showrooming' (browsing in high street stores but then searching for cheaper prices online) because they expect to find bargains on the internet.

Direct marketing – With the exception of personal selling, direct marketing (DM) is the promotional tool offering the most personalised form of communication. We use the term direct marketing to describe any form of personalised, direct communication with a customer or any other stakeholder.

Marketers can use a number of different channels and media to directly target the recipient of the message, including email, SMS, mail, telephone, direct response TV and direct selling. Ultimately, any channel through which you can deliver a message and call to action direct can be thought of as a direct marketing tool.

As technology develops, marketers will increasingly be able to use direct marketing to reach target consumers based on their digital behaviour and habits. They will know not only what consumers are looking for and when they are browsing, but also, via mobile devices, where they are when they do it. Digital also affords high levels of personalisation and tailoring in DM, making it a popular tool to support personal selling in B2B communications and campaigns.

Personal selling – This involves the use of a sales force to promote products and services, usually on a one-to-one basis. Because of the high cost per contact it is most appropriate in a business-to-business environment, or in selling complicated financial products. In such markets the product/service is complex, high value and needs careful explanation. The message can also be personalised immediately to the buyer's need.

Factors influencing the marketing communications mix
These can include the following:

Company resources – TV advertising, for example, is very expensive in terms of absolute costs, and for smaller companies it may not be a realistic option. Smaller companies tend to use direct mail, more localised campaigns, and, increasingly the internet.

Promotional objectives – Are you looking to differentiate your product or service from that offered by the competition? Consumer marketers may use TV advertising to achieve this, particularly if they need to reach a large audience. Business-to-business marketers are more likely to use personal selling to get their message across. Next time you're exposed to marketing and promotional messages and media give some consideration to what they're trying to achieve. What do you think their promotional objectives are?

How carefully the message needs to be controlled or managed – How important is the message? Advertising and sales promotion are very controllable, for example, whereas with PR you have very little control over what the media actually prints. A sales force can manage the message very carefully by personalising the message to each customer.

The level of credibility you want your audience to perceive – The public tends to see PR as the most credible marketing tool, particularly when an objective outsider is involved in the communication.

The nature and location of the target audience – Mass communication tools such as advertising are best suited to large, often international, consumer markets. B2B audiences, on the other hand, usually have complex decision-making units that are best targeted through personal selling.

Because promotional tools are rarely used in isolation marketers have to ensure that the mix of tools they select communicate the same message, clearly and consistently.

Buying behaviour and the promotional mix

As we discussed in Chapter 2.2 the **consumer purchase decision process** involves five stages:

1. Problem recognition
2. Information search
3. Evaluation of alternatives
4. Purchase decision
5. Post-purchase evaluation

Promotional tools play a part at each stage of this process. Sometimes they prompt a customer to recognise a need. At other times they provide information to help the customer make a choice. Potential purchasers may consult family and friends as part of their information search or evaluation process, and promotion can help by reminding these people of the benefits your product offers. In the post-purchase phase, a promotion may help to reassure customers that they made the right decision.

The factors that can influence the buying decision process are categorised as **personal** influences, **psychological** influences and **social** influences.

Let's use a car purchase to illustrate how some of these influences work in the consumer market.

Buying a car involves extensive decision-making because it's an expensive and infrequent investment. A car is a high-involvement purchase, and the potential customer will spend a lot of time and energy researching the market before making their final decision.

Other factors that influence the car-buying decision are:

- **Demographic** factors – In particular, age, sex, income and family life-cycle stage.
- **Situational** factors. For example, if the buyer has just started a new job and needs a car to travel to work, they may be under time pressure, so spend less time looking for information.

- **Psychological** factors, such as how the customer perceives the manufacturer in relation to the things that are important to him or her – safety or self-image, for example. Previous experience of a particular manufacturer will also exert a psychological influence.
- **Social influences** – Including the family, other reference groups (such as friends or work colleagues) and social class.

Marketers need to understand how these factors influence buyers so that they can shape their promotional offering to meet their needs.

Business-to-business customers also go through a buying decision process, and the stages are very similar to those in the consumer purchase decision process, as we outline below.

- **Recognition of problem** – Either a new purchase need or a re-purchase.
- **Development of product specifications to solve problem** – The end users of the product, together with technical specialists, will work to develop an appropriate specification. The internet may have helped the company to identify new ideas about how it could use the product, as it makes information more accessible to smaller companies.
- **Search for products and suppliers** – The internet can really help here. Previously, companies may have been limited to directories and local companies to find suppliers. Now they can search much more widely and use reverse auctions to request tenders.
- **Evaluate products and suppliers against specifications** – The company evaluates a shortlist of suppliers and products against the criteria it has set, or it considers and responds to tenders.
- **Select and order the most appropriate products** – Customers may give preference to suppliers with online purchase facilities.
- **Evaluate product and supplier performance** – The company considers whether the purchase was the best one and whether it worked. Because it has widened its choice it now has more power and could switch supplier much more easily, if it chose to.

Companies wishing to target SMEs need to ensure that their websites communicate appropriate benefits for SMEs, which increasingly search for suppliers online. Depending on the complexity of the product or service they offer, they may combine e-promotion with advertising in trade magazines (or on trade portals) and personal selling.

Digital media
Digital media have revolutionised many areas of promotion over the past few years, expanding the opportunities for marketers to communicate with their taget audiences and accelerating the development of relationship marketing. While digital has enhanced the communication between a company and its suppliers, its staff and its

customers, it has also raised the expectations of stakeholders, both internal and external, and marketers have to ensure they keep up with the new demands.

The new digital media are predominantly enabled by the internet, and provide new opportunities and channels for each of the five communications tools. We provide some examples below.

Advertising – The internet supports the delivery of a number of different types of advertising, from the classic banner ad and pop-ups to the more common interstitial adverts. Banner ads can also be used on other vehicles such as mobile apps and mobile-optimised websites. There are also paid-for display ads, via 'pay per click' on search engines, and targeted ads on social networks. Search engines also allow brands to advertise what they offer against that of competition in organic search results. Digital media can also be used to share viral adverts, the content of which needs to be funny, novel, entertaining, shocking – and highly relevant – to be effective.

Finally, word of mouth, one of the most powerful and most trusted forms of advertising, is highly influential online. Consumer generated media (CGM) associated with organisations, brands, products and services takes a number of different forms, including reviews, testimonials, social media posts and shared experiences on communities. All of them are an evolution of the word-of-mouth medium.

PR – Organisations can utilise digital media to share their message – via social media, via their website, even via their employees and their online channels. But negative PR is also highly visible online, as complaints, stories about poor treatment of customers and employees, and unethical practices (to name a few) are easily posted and shared – and can quickly go viral and reach a much larger, sometimes global, audience, causing significant damage to a brand.

But because messages can be shared so quickly and easily online, digital is the perfect medium for crisis response communications. In addition, 'press relations' sections on corporate websites afford journalists direct access to information, stories and contacts.

Sales promotion – Coupons, online-only deals, time-limited discounts and the like can all be delivered via the internet. The various online advertising and direct marketing channels available to marketers allow us to deliver sales promotions in a more timely and personalised manner than ever before. You can deliver them on your own website, via specialist voucher and coupon sites, via email and SMS, or even through developing technologies like iBeacons in stores, 'augmented reality' apps like Layar, or via Google Glass.

Direct marketing – The main channels that enable direct communications are SMS (or MMS), email, iBeacons (using Bluetooth), social media and display ads. Some of the messages, especially those delivered via email and SMS, are dismissed as 'spam' if they're unsolicited or intrusive, in the same way that direct mail can be perceived as 'junk mail'. Legislation controls this to some extent – via opt-in and opt-out options for example – but this has led to a new form of direct marketing – 'bacn' – direct emails that we (often inadvertently) sign up for via sites and when making purchases. They're not quite real messages, but not quite junk either, but it's safe to say that they are rarely read.

Personal selling – As mentioned earlier in the chapter, personal selling requires the buyer and seller to be present, and the immediacy and intimacy of the meeting are difficult to replicate online. Body language and other non-verbal signals are important elements in the buyer/seller relationship. However, 'online chats' or 'live chat' via digital media can be useful promotional tools in higher-involvement online purchases, and help to persuade interested customers to buy.

However, while digital media and tools play an integral role in the marketing mix, and especially the promotional mix, they should not be separated from more traditional marketing activities. Traditional and new media tools reinforce and add value to each other.

Packaging's role in promotion

As we discussed earlier in this chapter, packaging is said to fulfil four main functions – protection, promotion, provision of information and convenience. It is sometimes called 'the silent salesman' as, particularly for fast-moving consumer goods (FMCG), it is the only way of communicating brand image on the supermarket shelf.

For example, a company making healthy food products, such as Whole Earth, might use packaging to promote the brand and attract the eye. When Whole Earth's products were sold through specialist shops, it was competing directly with similar foods. Now that it is on supermarket shelves it faces indirect competition from 'non-health' foods and other goods.

Packaging also fulfils a communication role in that it provides information. Many countries (including the UK) have legislation stipulating the inclusion of certain information (the ingredients for example) on the packaging of foodstuffs. A brand like Whole Earth will also want to communicate its 'point of difference' – that is, natural ingredients, organically grown.

ACTIVITY 11

A medium-sized furniture manufacturer that sells direct to its target market is looking to move from providing basic home furnishings to designing and producing bespoke, durable office furniture on a business-to-business basis. Draw up a table like the one below and compare and contrast the marketing mix for the existing consumer market and the proposed business-to-business market.

	Home furnishings	Office furnishings
Product		
Price		
Place		
Promotion		

5.2 THE THREE ELEMENTS OF THE EXTENDED MARKETING MIX

The extended marketing mix for services consists of the four elements covered above – Product, Price, Place and Promotion – plus an additional three elements – People, Process and Physical Evidence – which take into account the differences between products and services. For example, products, or goods, are tangible and services are intangible. A service is not owned and it is consumed at the point of exchange – it can't be taken away. It can also be much harder to standardise quality in a service experience than it is for a mass-produced product.

Let's look at the additional three elements in the extended marketing mix.

People – You need people with the attitudes and skills to enable them to deal professionally with customers. People form part of the service offered, and are a big determinant of customer satisfaction (or dissatisfaction).

Process – You need to ensure that the systems and processes involved in delivering the service are sufficiently robust and effective to ensure that you deliver a consistently professional approach. Examples include appointment and queuing systems. How quickly can the customer get an appointment to see the dentist or the bank manager? How long do people stand in a queue before more staff are deployed to serve them? Is this acceptable to customers? Process is also an important factor in online interactions and transactions. How easy is it to find information on a website, and how easy and secure is the process when making an online purchase for example?

Physical evidence – This is often referred to as the 'ambience' of the environment in which the service is offered. It includes things such as layout, décor, noise, appearance, smell and ease of access.

Let's consider the way that a football or rugby team might develop an extended marketing mix for its 'service'.

Product – The service is the game the spectators watch.

Price – There is normally some form of price differentiation – regular customers pay less than occasional spectators, for example. You can't store unused seats or sell them off cheaply at the end of the day, as you can with food, but season tickets help deal with the 'perishability' aspect of this particular sporting service.

Promotion – You could use several promotional tools:

- Advertising – TV commercials, merchandising to build the brand.
- PR – around new players that are signed, and the approach to the game.

- Personal selling – of tickets on site.
- Direct marketing – letter, email or text reminders of upcoming games and events.
- Sales promotion – free admission for children accompanied by their parents at selected matches to encourage family attendance.

Place – Where and how accessible is the stadium? What facilities does it have? Are travel facilities provided when the team is playing away?

People – The quality of the service is directly related to the people that deliver it. Customer service is very important in sports, and volunteers often help to deliver it – think about the contribution the Games Makers added to the experience of London 2012. Management needs to treat volunteers and employees well to ensure that customer service standards are consistently high. They need to treat their players well too, as they are the ones providing the entertainment and excitement that is at the core of the service offered.

Process – The 'process' used to purchase tickets, or obtain refunds, for example, must be efficient to keep customers happy. This applies whether the process is online or handled in person at the stadium. The 'process' people go through when entering the stadium, finding their seats, using the facilities and so on all has to be designed with the customer in mind.

Physical evidence – The environment within the stadium must be appropriate. Many football stadiums use the team colours in the seating areas. Cleanliness and safety are the most important factors for this sort of service. Much of the ambience is provided by the fans themselves. Programmes can provide a valued memento of the game, particularly for high status games such as cup competitions.

5.3

THE IMPORTANCE OF A CO-ORDINATED APPROACH TO THE MARKETING MIX

A marketing mix needs to be co-ordinated – that is, all elements of the mix have work together effectively. Some marketing theory suggests that the mix needs to be 'synergistic' so that the elements of the mix employed work together to deliver an enhanced result, greater than the sum of the parts involved. In practice, however, there are limits to what marketers can change, and how quickly.

The target market, and its needs, wants, desires and behaviours, is, or should be, a major influence on the content of the marketing mix. Marketers will arrive at the most appropriate mix based on data gathered from the marketing environment and marketing research, analysed and turned into insight. All of the elements must create value for the target market, satisfy (or even delight) it, and deliver on the marketing, business and corporate objectives.

For example, if we know our target market shops in a particular store, or is based in a certain geographic area, we can adapt the 'place' elements of the mix accordingly. If we know our target market reads a particular newspaper, or browses particular websites, then we can ensure our message is delivered via these channels and media at relevant times.

The components of the mix need to be compatible with each other, they need to support and add value to each other within the mix, and they need to make sense to the target market. An expensive and poor quality product available only in exclusive, luxury retailers won't last very long. Equally, a great service, but with little or no promotion or an irrelevant advertising campaign, won't be noticed or understood.

In conclusion, you have to develop each element of the mix with the other elements in mind, as well the position you would like the product, service or idea to occupy in the market and in the minds of your target audience.

CASE STUDY

Mitie is a facilities management (FM) company operating in the B2B market. It's recently been through a major rebranding exercise aimed at aligning the brand with the company ethos – that is, a focus on partnerships with customers, suppliers, the community and staff.

You can see the key elements of Mitie's marketing mix on its website: www.mitie.com. Have a look at its strategy and culture, and see how it's developed to support the people and process elements of the mix. The site itself is a great example of promotion, and has further examples within it, such as social media and PR.

This is a good example of a co-ordinated marketing mix, where all elements work together to provide synergy.

ACTIVITY 12

Think about the last time you consumed a service rather than a tangible product. This may have been a visit to the cinema or theatre, or a sports event, or you may have been seeking advice about a financial issue.

Make notes on the marketing mix that is in place for this service, identifying all '7Ps'.

QUICK QUIZ – CHECK YOUR KNOWLEDGE

1. With which element of the 'total product concept' (core, actual and augmented) would the installation of a new cable TV box best fit?
   a. core
   b. actual
   c. augmented
   d. potential

2. Which two stages of the buyer decision-making process are specific to B2B decisions?
   a. Recognition of problem and evaluation of alternatives.
   b. Supplier search and post-purchase evaluation.
   c. Product specification and supplier search.
   d. Purchase and post-purchase evaluation.

3. Which of the following are components of a service but not a product?

>   **(1)** Intangibility.
>   **(2)** Price.
>   **(3)** Benefits.
>   **(4)** Not possible to own.

>   **a.** 1 and 4
>   **b.** 2 and 3
>   **c.** 3 and 4
>   **d.** 1 and 2

4. A co-ordinated marketing mix is an important concept within marketing tactics as it provides:
>   **a.** Fragmentation.
>   **b.** Synergy.
>   **c.** Confusion.
>   **d.** Innovation .

(Answers: 1:c, 2:c, 3:a, 4:b)

6.

MEETING CUSTOMER NEEDS THROUGH THE MARKETING MIX

OUTLINE

In this chapter we will look in more depth at how the marketing mix can be adapted to different contexts, including small and medium-sized enterprises (SMEs), not-for-profit organisations and international companies, as well as business-to-consumer and business-to-business organisations. We will also consider how the mix might be put together to build relationships with customers and how changes in the environment affect a marketing mix. Finally, we consider the important role of monitoring and measuring success.

At the end of this chapter you will be able to:

- Recommend a marketing mix for products and services.
- Recommend a marketing mix in different contexts.
- Explain how to adapt the marketing mix to changes in the environment in order to keep customers satisfied.
- Recommend how to measure and control the effectiveness of the marketing mix.

DEFINITIONS

Business-to-business (B2B) – Relating to the sale of a product or service for any use other than personal consumption. The buyer may be a manufacturer, a reseller, a government body, a not-for-profit organisation etc.

Business-to-consumer (B2C) – Relating to the sale of products or services for personal consumption. The buyer may be an individual, family or other group, buying to use the product themselves or for someone else to use.

Fast-moving consumer goods (FMCG) – These include packaged food, beverages, toiletries and tobacco.

Not for profit/third sector – The charity and voluntary sector. Objectives are different from those in commercial organisations, but marketing is still relevant.

'Objective and task' approach – Considers the objective of the campaign, sets out tasks needed to achieve it and costs for each task (to arrive at total budget required).

Relationship marketing – The strategy of establishing a relationship with the customer, which continues well beyond the first purchase.

Small to medium-sized enterprise (SME) – Usually defined as organisations with fewer than 250 employees. Medium-sized businesses have 50 to 249 employees and small businesses have up to 49 employees. Small businesses include micro businesses, which can be separately defined as having up to five employees.

THE MARKETING MIX FOR PRODUCTS AND SERVICES

In the previous chapter, we saw a detailed explanation of each element of the 7P marketing mix, along with some examples. This chapter will look at the way the marketing mix is co-ordinated in different types of organisations and to meet various objectives.

We have seen the way that 4Ps developed into 7Ps. This was originally because services were recognised as being different from tangible products. However, as markets become more competitive, marketers look for new ways to add value to their products, and so all 7Ps have become an appropriate mix for every marketer, whether they are working with products or services.

The marketing mix is the tactical activity that puts into practice the strategy designed to meet marketing objectives. You have to design the marketing mix with the marketing objectives in mind. For example, if the objective is to grow market share over a relatively short period of time, then pricing products or services too high won't work. But it's equally important not to drop the price too low or it will adversely affect customers' perceptions of quality.

So developing an appropriate marketing mix is not easy. You have to put it together in a way that meets organisational objectives and the needs of the target segment. It is not unusual for organisations to use different marketing mixes for different target markets, and this is known as 'differentiated targeting'.

At the end of the previous chapter we explored why it is important to co-ordinate all elements of the mix to get maximum benefit from marketing campaigns. The make-up of the mix is driven by the nature of the target audience, the desired positioning in the minds of target customers, the marketing objectives and the industry sector in which the organisation operates.

But marketing is not only concerned with attracting new business or acquiring new customers; it is also about building and maintaining relationships too. It has to meet (and sometimes prompt) customer's needs and set and meet their expectations of product and service quality. Here again, the marketing mix is the toolkit the marketer uses to do this.

In this chapter we will explore how to adapt the marketing mix to take into account all these different factors.

6.2

The business-to-consumer marketing mix

Marketers need to differentiate their offering from that of their competitors.

Imagine you want to buy a television. What size screen will you need? Will it go on the wall or stand on a table? Do you want a flat or curved screen? How much are you prepared to pay? Where will you buy it? Will it be an online retailer such as Amazon? Or would you prefer to shop in a department store such as John Lewis? Where will you find information about TVs? Will you look online or in a magazine?

The answers to these questions will shape your decision about who you buy from, and that company's marketing mix will determine your choice. The business-to-consumer marketing mix is usually the easiest for marketers to understand because they, after all, are consumers too and have lots of personal experience and examples to draw on.

You need to use research and development to ensure that the products or 'bundles of benefits' you offer continue to meet the needs of customers, and then build a marketing mix around that bundle of benefits to keep customers satisfied and loyal.

The business-to-business marketing mix

Differences between the marketing mix for business-to-business and business-to-consumer (B2C) marketers are driven by the different characteristics of the products they supply, and by the different buyer behaviour.

In Chapter 2 we saw that business-to-business (B2B) marketing can be categorised by the nature of the purchase. This in turn will affect the complexity of the decision-making unit (in consumer marketing it might just be one individual, whereas in B2B marketing a number of different functions are likely to be represented) and the length of the buying process.

There are three main purchase types to consider:

- New-task purchase.
- Modified re-buy.
- Straight re-buy.

The marketing mix for each of these three types of purchase will differ, because of the nature of the purchase being made.

New tasks – Tend to be major purchases, with a complex decision-making unit (DMU) involved and a long lead-time before the purchase is made. They *can* be less complex though – like buying paper from a new stationery supplier.

Modified re-buys – Will be simpler, provided the original product or service has met expectations. Customers may want faster delivery, or a modification to the product. In this case personal selling will be particularly useful, as negotiations and a personalised approach are required.

Straight re-buys – Occur when businesses are re-ordering fairly straightforward products, such as consumables for use in the business or standard components for use in manufacturing their own products.

The B2B marketing mix typically differs from the B2C mix in the following ways:

Product – It is just as important for business-to-business marketers to differentiate their offering from those of their competitors as it is for consumer marketers. But the products supplied are often more complex than consumer products and are much more likely to include service both before and after the sale takes place. For example, technical advice may be provided before the sale, and user training afterwards.

Price – There is often more negotiation involved in decisions about price in business-to-business markets. In addition, some companies require suppliers to 'bid' for business by set dates. Using the internet, some organisations are now using reverse auctions to request tenders for business. Bidders at these auctions undercut each other for the privilege of winning the tender.

Place – Distribution channels for industrial goods tend to be shorter than those for consumer goods. Many companies supply their products direct to the user company, using their own sales force to complete the business. Issues such as transport arrangements, storage of products and inventory control are all important to these companies.

Promotion – The promotional mix for business-to-business markets differs from that in consumer markets in several ways. Some businesses supply a few major customers, making the use of personal selling much more feasible. Products and services are often quite complex, and they are more easily explained by a sales person face to face than through a 'blanket' approach in printed media. The buying unit within the customer organisation can also be complex, and the sales person needs to develop relationships with the decision-makers, adapting the message to address individual concerns. Advertising is often limited to appropriate trade journals and magazines, and usually has a more logical than emotional message.

Many B2B organisations are now seeing the benefit of a social media presence. For example, Norbar Torque Tools adopted @voiceoftorque as its Twitter user name or 'handle', and positioned itself as *the* place to ask questions about anything to do with torque. These days, it is reckoned that much of the pre-sale work in B2B marketing happens before the sales person gets involved, through website searches, search engine optimisation (SEO), LinkedIn, Twitter and so on.

People – The 'people' element of the marketing mix is very important in business-to-business marketing. As we've already discussed, products and services tend to be much more complex and many companies supply just a few major customers, making personal selling, often by specialists (in, for example, pharmaceuticals or engineering), a highly effective tool. People build empathy with clients and through sustained relationships can win loyalty.

Process – The processes involved in getting products and services to business customers are also important, and marketers need to consider them when first drawing up the terms and conditions of sale. A true company-wide market orientation is critical to getting the processes right, as we pointed out in Chapter 2, and internal marketing plays an important role here in ensuring that everyone involved in these processes 'thinks customer first'.

Physical evidence – Corporate branding, signs and symbols are particularly important in B2B marketing to build the credibility and trust that encourage customers to buy on an ongoing basis.

SME marketing

SMEs are usually limited in their growth opportunities by financial constraints, and as a result tend to start off as more 'hands-on' market oriented than most. The owner, or a small number of staff, get to know their customers personally, and regular dialogue with them helps the company keep pace with their changing needs. With just a few key customers, and the owner's active involvement with them, the company can very quickly adapt its product or service or adjust the price because the decision-making chain is so short.

SMEs keep distribution strategies simple, and they tackle promotion on an 'all we can afford' basis.

As the organisation grows, however, the owner can no longer do all the sales and marketing himself or herself, so recruits one or more sales staff. Because the initial marketing approach was informal, and often unplanned, the organisation *thinks* it is still very customer focused. But it is often a sales-driven organisation that emerges, driven by short-term targets rather than a market orientation.

Due to what are typically lower resource levels, SMEs need to tailor the marketing mix to play to their strengths.

Product – Small businesses can often succeed by finding a market niche through which they can differentiate themselves from larger competitors. But while they may start off with a very flexible approach to customising the product, as they grow this can turn into an assumption that they are customer focused simply because they are communicating the benefits of the product to customers.

Price – If a small business is trying to sell to large buyers, it may find it difficult to convince them of its reliability and financial stability. Clear pricing structures based on what the market will stand will help it make its case.

Place – Many SMEs deal directly with their customers, embracing new channels to market only when they become established. At that point they need to think about things like the products they offer, the channels their competitors use, and how the costs of each potential new channel might affect the prices they have to charge.

Promotion – This will be restricted by the amount of budget available and by the owner's approach to setting the budget. If the owner takes an 'objective and task' approach to setting the promotional budget then the marketer is likely to be able to put together a co-ordinated promotional plan. They're unlikely to use TV advertising though because of the high costs involved. SMEs often use digital marketing and social media tactically, as they view these as a 'cheaper' form of promotion (although when they actually measure the amount of time and resource they use in maintaining a digital presence they are often surprised by the true costs). Digital and social media also allow small businesses to have a greater geographic 'reach' – provided they have an appropriate product and can manage the logistics of getting products to international customers.

People – This is potentially an area of difficulty for a small business, particularly as it grows. Customers get used to dealing with one person, typically the owner, and after what could be years of personal contact with him or her don't take kindly to an unknown successor – particularly one less senior. They may feel less supported than previously. This situation needs careful handling to ensure that loyal customers don't defect to a competitor.

Process – This element of the mix too can cause problems for a fast-growing small business. As it grows it needs new processes, but lack of resources can mean that these have to go through various stages of development and can't keep up with what customers want, leading to frustration and disappointment.

Physical evidence – The key word under this element of the mix, particularly for SMEs, is consistency. As a small business develops its knowledge of marketing, there is a danger that it introduces a whole array of marketing and promotional materials with a mix of different imagery, logos and content.

The not-for-profit/third sector marketing mix

In the past many people thought that marketing could only be applied to the world of business, and in sectors such as not-for-profit some deemed it positively inappropriate. That's all changed, and marketing is now used successfully in charities, local government, schools, political parties, hospitals, churches, museums etc.

The main difference between not-for-profit marketing and commercial marketing is the objectives they are looking to achieve. Businesses exist primarily to satisfy the needs of shareholders, by increasing the value of their investments in the business. Not-for-profit organisations serve a different group of stakeholders – the beneficiaries of a charity or residents in a housing association, for example, whose needs are typically met by a service rather than financial gain.

Just as organisational objectives differ, so the marketing mix differs in such organisations.

Product – Some not-for-profit organisations create physical products to sell to raise funds. For example, museums sell mementos and leisure services may sell sports equipment and clothing. More often than not, the not-for-profit organisation is marketing a service, and so the basic service marketing characteristics apply to them, just as they do to profit-making businesses.

Price – Prices are 'set' on a very different basis in the not-for-profit sector. For example, the prices a local council leisure centre charges might not cover the cost of running the service. The lower prices might be part of a package designed to benefit the local community and be supplemented by local taxes.

Place – In recent years there have been changes in 'place' decisions, particularly for charities, many of which now sell made or donated goods from high street shops to raise funds.

Promotion – A combination of financial constraints and stakeholders' perception that marketing is 'wasting' valuable resources that should instead go to ' the cause', serves to limit marketing expenditure. However, image is very important for these organisations, who operate in an increasingly competitive 'market'. Some national charities now use highly targeted campaigns with emotional messages to encourage donations.

When communicating with its 'publics', any organisation must ensure that it is sending appropriate messages. A charity's audiences include existing and potential donors, supporters, collectors and so on, and it needs to consider the potential reactions of all its stakeholders when putting together a promotional mix. For example, 'guerrilla marketing stunts' create awareness, and, if done correctly, can make quite an impact, helping to attract funds from new donors in particular. However, the charity would need to forecast the results of the activity very carefully (more carefully perhaps than a commercial organisation), as regular donors would take a dim view of their donations being used to fund a stunt that does not break even. Unfortunately, unlike other forms of promotion that can be pre-tested, this type of event relies to some extent on the element of 'surprise', so the impact would be lost if a 'test' was carried out.

Planners need to carefully consider the cost of the stunt, forecast the likely return, and communicate the plan to relevant stakeholders in a way that reassures them while not undermining the impact of the stunt.

CASE STUDY
A few years ago the World Wildlife Fund (WWF) wanted to raise awareness of how few pandas are left in the world. They put 1,600 papier-mâché pandas in front of the Eiffel Tower. The stunt certainly raised awareness, but was it appropriate and a good use of the charity's money?

The international marketing mix
International marketing exists in many forms. It can involve a relatively small firm looking to extend its market by exporting a few products to another country, or it can be a large company, such as Coca-Cola, standardising its marketing mix and operating globally. The internet is, in some cases, making it easier to do business internationally.

The choices available to companies looking to operate in international markets are as follows:

1. Use the same marketing mix worldwide – a 'global' mix.
2. Adapt the promotional mix, but standardise the product. This keeps costs down by offering the same product mix, but you can tailor advertising to take account of cultural and language differences.
3. Adapt the product, but standardise promotion. In the car market, for example, manufacturers adapt models to comply with the different countries' laws regarding emission levels.
4. Adapt both product and promotion. Sometimes the product is adapted and consumers need to be informed of this fact through adapted promotion.
5. Introduce new products for different international environments.

Important differences when marketing across borders

The marketing mix is a useful framework for considering the differences in international markets that may affect the way marketing is approached. Marketers need to take careful account of the different external environments (using the PESTELE framework, or similar, that we discussed in Chapter 3) when developing each element of the mix.

Product – National culture is the main difference to consider when marketing products abroad. Factors such as climate, the local economy, and even the electricity supply may also affect the product itself.

Price – Exchange rates will have an impact on pricing decisions, as well as what the local market is prepared to pay for a product. There are also additional costs involved in transporting products internationally.

Place – The infrastructure within other countries, and distribution systems generally, will vary from country to country.

Promotion – Cultural and language differences are the main considerations, as well as the availability and cost of media.

People – You need to recruit customer contact staff very carefully. If you use staff from your home market they may have problems with the culture and/or language. If you recruit from the local market it may be more difficult to motivate and manage them.

Process – The processes that are standard for you in your home market may not be appropriate internationally. You need to do marketing research to check.

Physical evidence – Again, what is acceptable and expected in the home market may not be what customers accept and expect in an international market.

A marketing mix to build relationships

As we mentioned at the beginning of this chapter, there has been a marked shift from transaction-based to relationship-based marketing. The relationship marketing concept is based on the theory that organisations can enjoy relationships with customers similar to those that exist between individuals.

In transactional marketing, each sale is seen in isolation, and is carried out with no regard to previous or potential future business. Relationship marketing, on the other hand, takes into account the impact of every business encounter on the existing relationship and the likely consequences for any future business. The aim is to attract and retain customers, because, as we noted earlier, loyal customers are more profitable.

It's now accepted that long-term relationships are essential for a business's performance and survival. Traditional selling techniques aimed to get that first or single sale, neglecting any possibility of repeat business. But in most industries these days, the relationship between buyer and seller doesn't end once a single transaction has taken place. Modern selling techniques are based on developing partnerships and relationships with customers to foster long-term business, bringing the sales ethos into closer alignment with marketing.

We can describe relationship marketing as all the activities that an organisation uses to build, maintain and enhance customer relations. This means that marketers are increasingly concerned not just with the marketing mix, but also with customer service and quality issues.

Relationship marketing was originally used in B2B marketing and in services. It has now spread into consumer goods markets, especially as these have been enhanced with value-added services. Relationship marketing has developed because of the growing need to differentiate products and services to counter price-based competition. It can lend an organisation real and sustainable competitive advantage in an increasingly complex marketplace.

Marketers can adapt the marketing mix to ensure they build lasting relationships in whatever market they operate in using some of the following approaches.

Consumer markets – Technology such as the internet, email and data mining software has enabled companies to build one-to-one relationships with their customers. There are different permutations of relationship marketing, including 'loyalty marketing' – that is cards and points systems that reward regular customers. In addition, social media now allows organisations and customers to engage with each other on a 24/7 basis. This is extremely time-consuming however, and organisations with many customers will find it difficult to have 'personal' relationships with even a fraction of their customer base.

B2B markets – In business-to-business marketing, long-term relationships are very important. Buyers and sellers often meet regularly to share information and work together to find mutually beneficial solutions to problems. Developing specifications and negotiating over price can be a lengthy process, requiring a number of meetings between the two different parties. Developing long-term relationships is beneficial to both sides because it means they are aware of each other's needs and capabilities.

Service markets – Relationship marketing is critical in service marketing. Due to the inseparable and intangible nature of services, the customer's satisfaction and perception of the company relies heavily on the attitude and appearance of the person providing the service. Frequently, the customer is purchasing the personal qualities and skills of the service provider, so the ability to develop close relationships and win customer confidence is crucial.

Successful relationships

Effective relationship marketing depends on the following elements:

- Development of core service (Product).
- Core products or services augmented with extra benefits (Product).
- Relationship customised to individual's needs (Promotion).
- Pricing that encourages loyalty (Price).
- Marketing to employees (People).
- Use of two-way communication (Promotion).
- Trust, warmth, commitment, intimacy, honesty and respect (Co-ordinated mix).
- Awareness of all stakeholders (Co-ordinated mix).

Key account management (KAM) is a highly important concept for companies operating in business-to-business or service markets, where the customers are other organisations, or, in some circumstances, wealthy individuals.

Companies will identify that some of their customers are more valuable than others and these are generally termed 'key customers', but are also known as key accounts, major accounts and national accounts. Organisations tend to manage these important customers separately from the rest of the customer base. The process of managing them is sometimes considered within channel management or distribution strategies, especially where key accounts are wholesalers or other distributors.

Key account management processes are the activities, mechanisms and procedures that enable a company to manage its key customers effectively.

ACTIVITY 13

How much do you know about internet advertising and the law, in particular data protection legislation covering the way personal information is stored and used?

Search on the internet for information that provides guidance to organisations on how to use digital communications to build relationships with customers.

6.3

ADAPTING THE MARKETING MIX TO CHANGING ENVIRONMENTS

We saw in Chapter 3 that the marketing environment is constantly changing, and, in Chapter 5, that marketing and the marketing mix need to be dynamic to keep pace. A variety of factors within the macro and micro marketing environments can affect marketing, and it's increasingly important to be able to adapt and flex the approach to keep up with increasingly rapid changes in those environments in order to develop or maintain a sustainable competitive advantage.

Some changes can have a significant, even damaging, impact on the organisation – consider the number of retail businesses (Woolworths, HMV and Blockbuster for example) that have gone into administration in recent years due to their failure to adapt, or adapt quickly enough, to the changing environmental conditions.

Some organisations are more proactive, and instead of monitoring and responding to change, they instigate change in the marketing environment. These organisations can be quite aggressive and seek to define the marketplace they operate in. They are often referred to as 'market drivers' as opposed to being 'market driven'.

Changing macro and micro factors

As we identified in Chapter 3, the factors within the macro environment are outside the organisation's control, and the PESTELE framework (or any similar variation) is a useful tool for identifying and analysing the impact, influence and importance of these factors in relation to the marketplace, competition and the target markets. These macro factors present marketers with opportunities and/or threats, depending on how they choose to respond.

Micro-environmental factors are more connected to the organisation itself and affect its ability to create and deliver value. The key players, or stakeholders, within the micro environment include customers, competitors, suppliers, intermediaries, governments and pressure groups – in short, any stakeholder or 'public' that is interested in, or affected by, the organisation.

The macro and micro environments are interlinked. Macro-environmental factors can have a significant impact on competition, on customers' behaviour, needs and wants, and on the attitudes of the general public. Marketers have two key methods to monitor, gather data and develop information and insights on these two changing environments – marketing research and market intelligence.

The macro environment

To recap, the models available to gather data from and analyse the macro environment include PEST (Political, Economic, Social and Technological), which is the simplest, and PESTELE, which adds

Environmental, Legal and Ethical to the model. The model you use is largely irrelevant; far more important is to consider the factors intelligently and analyse their impact, influence and importance in order to help you make informed decisions.

Economic factors – Organisations are likely to be affected by both national and global economic changes. Economies go through cycles, which typically include four stages – boom, slowdown, recession and recovery – although the length of time each stage takes can vary. Increasingly, the economy is becoming 'global' as the recent global financial crisis demonstrated. The economy can affect inflation, employment, disposable income, credit, tax and duties.

Social factors – The attitudes and behaviour of the population have changed significantly over recent years, influenced in no small part by changes in technology, the economy and even the natural environment. The global population has grown significantly, populations are ageing (as people live much longer), middle classes are burgeoning, and lifestyle, social interactions, working practices and purchasing behaviour are being transformed. These are just a few of the social changes over the past 50 years that affect marketing.

Political factors – These are predominantly associated with the governments of countries where organisations operate. The government in power has a direct impact on a business's operations (in terms of laws, policies, funding, imports and exports etc) but it also has an indirect effect through its impact on the overall economy. Companies will be influenced by governments in every country they operate in.

Technological factors – These have had a significant impact on markets, people and society as well as on organisations' operations and processes. This area of the macro environment is perhaps the most dynamic, especially over the past few decades. Computers and processors are smaller and more powerful, there are new and improved products and services (EInk, flexible displays, 4G and graphene are just a few examples), and connectivity via fixed and wireless networks has improved dramatically. Organisations that are receptive to change have thrived, whereas others have been significantly disrupted or even put out of business.

The micro environment
There are two main elements to consider here – competitors and customers.

Changes in competition – A key factor of the micro environment is competition. Almost every organisation operates in a competitive environment, although the intensity of competitive rivalry varies between different industries. And the nature of competition has changed. Key competitors used to be considered as those that offered similar products or services – so 'direct' competitors. Now the biggest threat, arguably, is 'indirect' competitors – essentially any organisation that is targeting a similar segment to you – because these days organisations are competing for consumers' spend or attention, whatever the nature of their offer.

For example, a cinema, gym, pub and nightclub may not be direct competitors, but they are all competing for the same 'leisure pound' from consumers.

Technology has also facilitated an increase in what we call 'substitute competition'. Digital products have 'de-materialised' many products that used to exist only in tangible form. So, for example, cinemas now compete with streaming services such as Netflix or other film-on-demand services, and they may even be competing with illegal streaming and torrent sites. Books, CDs, films and mail are all examples of products that have been de-materialised due to technological developments, and 3D printing, as it becomes more efficient and accessible, could take de-materialisation to another level.

Customer trends – Customers are influenced by internal factors – attitudes, motivations, personality and learning, for example – and external factors – culture, family, friends, role models and 'aspirant groups'.

Marketers can be instrumental in setting trends, but often we end up following them. Trend-setting organisations are known as 'market drivers', as we mentioned earlier in this section.

Recent customer trends have been influenced by technology, celebrity culture and the global financial crisis.

Technology has transformed customers' purchasing behaviour, including how they become aware of products, how they search for information, how they evaluate and buy products, and how they share their opinions and experiences.

The celebrity culture is linked to aspirant groups, and primarily affects younger audiences. It influences what they do, what they aspire to be and, of course, what brands they purchase.

The financial crisis promoted a change in purchasing, especially in relation to FMCG goods. Discount stores in the UK grew significantly as consumers changed their supermarket shopping habits, and this had a negative impact on some of the 'Big Four' supermarkets.

CASE STUDY

One customer trend that has emerged recently is 'dual-screening'. Research indicates that TV viewers are significantly more engaged with the events taking place on the screen if they are using a mobile device at the same time to comment on the events via social media or text.

Recent research shows that 60 per cent of Twitter users in the UK tweet about soaps, talent shows, reality shows and sporting events as they watch them. This has led to a number of shows developing 'hashtags' (for example #GBBO for the Great British Bake Off) so that the social media comments have a wider reach and can be better monitored. It can also enable the shows, TV channels, celebrities, sports stars and even brands in the shows to engage with audiences at a time when they are more receptive.

Keeping customers satisfied

Through marketing research and market intelligence, marketers can start to develop a better understanding of the changing marketing environment and use this to adapt the marketing mix. Speed is of the essence: the quicker you can react and adapt the better.

If things don't improve as a result of changing the marketing mix, then you may need to revisit and adapt the marketing strategy, or even the marketing objectives.

But the mix is usually the first element of the marketing plan to be adapted, depending on what the research and intelligence throws up. Some areas of the mix might be difficult to flex: for example, a dramatic price change is not advisable, nor are knee-jerk changes to products or distributors. But you can change promotion and the extended marketing mix relatively easily, although there will inevitably be associated work and costs involved.

The marketing mix, as we discussed earlier in this chapter and in Chapter 5, is a set of tools that marketers can use to create and deliver value for target markets. You need to consider any proposed change to the mix in relation to its impact on the customer. This impact may not always be positive. For example, if legislative changes in the macro environment mean packaging has to change, this may necessitate a minor price increase. However, you can use the promotional mix to minimise any potential negative impact and make the target market aware of the benefits of the change.

There is no magic formula as to what to change in the mix, or when, to counter changes in the external environment. Marketers have to rely on research and intelligence to make informed decisions. However, the value of previous experience shouldn't be under-estimated either: marketers who use knowledge and learning gained from earlier changes can build a strong bank of skills and market understanding to draw on to help inform future decisions on the most appropriate marketing mix.

6.4

MEASURING THE EFFECTIVENESS OF THE MARKETING MIX

The final and very important stage of the marketing planning process is to review performance against objectives. If the objectives are measurable, then this part of the process is much easier, because the marketer can look at overall performance against objectives to determine how effective, efficient and profitable activity has been.

Measuring the effectiveness of marketing is an important issue for the profession generally. Many of you will be familiar with the much-repeated saying from John Wanamaker, who is considered the father of both the modern department store and modern advertising:
"I know that half of my advertising dollars are wasted.... I just don't know which half."

But in today's cost-conscious organisations, marketers are expected to be increasingly accountable and to justify their expenditure on creating awareness and winning and retaining customers. Indeed, the marketing profession as a whole has a responsibility to demonstrate the effectiveness of marketing and its contribution to the bottom line. And this, of course, is about justifying their own existence too.

The good news is that the number of tools and techniques available to measure marketing is growing, and they are both quantitative and qualitative in nature.

Let's look at some examples, linked to each of the 4Ps.

1. PRODUCT

Sales analysis – Comparison of sales volume and value against forecasts, industry norms and competitors.

Cost analysis – Breaks down the costs of the marketing activities to see what each has achieved and which have been the most effective.

You can carry out the combination of sales and cost analysis by product, product line, segment, region or individual marketing channel, so these measurement techniques also fit under 'Place' and 'Promotion'.

Market share – Measuring sales volume can give a good indication of market share growth. If we know the percentage share we hold at the beginning of the year we can measure growth as a result of various marketing activities.

Number of new products developed and successfully launched – If our objectives are to grow through new product development, or to innovate better or faster than the competition, then the number of new products developed might be a suitable measure of success.

Repeat purchases – If we are putting together a marketing mix to retain customers through relationship marketing, then repeat purchases (as opposed to acquiring new customers) is an appropriate measure.

2. PRICE

Margin – What margin is achieved on each sale? This is very relevant in business-to-business marketing and in the selling of 'solutions', where there is no fixed price and an element of negotiation is involved.

Discount levels – Once again, this is common in business-to-business marketing. Sales people may be given guidelines as to how much discount is available, and this may increase by sales volume.

Comparisons with competitors – When a product or service is carefully positioned in the mind of customers, then the price must maintain that positioning. Ongoing comparisons of competitor prices are important in achieving this.

3. PROMOTION

Brand awareness – How much has awareness improved as a result of particular marketing campaigns?

Media coverage – How much positive PR coverage have we had across various media? This is usually measured in 'column inches'. In other words, how much would it have cost to buy the same amount of advertising space?

Cost per contact – TV advertising is expensive in real terms. However, it is probably seen by thousands more people than an advertisement in a specialist magazine. The 'cost per contact' compares this cost.

Sales/call ratios – In personal selling, this is a common measure. You can measure both the volume and value of sales achieved, and measure these against the number of calls made.

Enquiries generated – The number of enquiries or leads generated can help measure the success of a campaign or a trade exhibition.

4. PLACE

Costs – The costs associated with using one channel compared to another will be a factor in the overall profitability of the business. For example, are costs highest using intermediaries, using own-branded retailers or through e-commerce?

Volume of sales – When considering whether to maintain a particular channel, it may be relevant to compare the volume of sales achieved through that channel with those achieved through e-commerce or other alternatives. However, volume of sales is not the only consideration, as a channel may provide other services to customers unrelated to sales.

Business growth – If this is an objective of the company, then it cascades down to the channel used.

Stock levels – If a channel doesn't maintain sufficient stock this can affect customer satisfaction and, in turn, the brand.

Complaints – The number of complaints you receive about specific channels may be a factor in your decision to rationalise it.

Customer satisfaction – How well have levels been maintained over the year through each of the channels used, or by channel member (that is, agent, distributor, wholesaler or retailer)? This too can help inform decisions about which channels to use in the future.

Repeating the detailed marketing audit can also help you review marketing effectiveness, particularly if it includes measurable objectives.

ACTIVITY 14

Research ways that different organisations measure customer satisfaction. Make a list of the various methods used, and decide which would be the most appropriate for your organisation.

QUICK QUIZ – CHECK YOUR KNOWLEDGE

1. Which of the following is the best description of a modified re-buy in business-to-business marketing?
   a. A purchase made by an organisation for the first time.
   b. A purchase the organisation has made before, but from a different company.
   c. A purchase the organisation has made before, but this time they have changed the volume and/or slightly altered the specification.
   d. A purchase made by an organisation that has been made before.

2. The group of people involved in making a purchase decision is referred to as:
   a. A focus group.
   b. A decision-making process.
   c. A buying behaviour group.
   d. A decision-making unit.

3. Comparison of sales volume to forecasts is a form of:
   a. Sales analysis.
   b. Cost analysis.
   c. Profit analysis.
   d. Market analysis.

4. Making a comparison with competitors is most likely to be a measure used in which element of the marketing mix?
   a. Product.
   b. Price.
   c. Place.
   d. Promotion.

(Answers: 1:c, 2:d, 3:a, 4:b)

GLOSSARY

Business-to-business (B2B) – Relating to the sale of a product or service for any use other than personal consumption. The buyer may be a manufacturer, a reseller, a government body, a non-profit-making institution, or any organisation other than an ultimate consumer.

Business-to-consumer (B2C) – Relating to the sale of products or services for personal consumption. The buyer may be an individual, family or other group, buying to use the product themselves, or for someone else to use.

Competencies – An organisation's core competencies are the functional capabilities the organisation uses on a continuing basis to achieve its mission or strategic goals.

Consumer behaviour – The buying habits and patterns of consumers in the acquisition and use of products and services.

Consumer buying decision-making process – The process that consumers go through when making a purchase decision.

Co-ordinated mix – The elements of the 7P marketing mix designed and implemented to support and add value to each other.

Corporate governance – The processes, systems and principles by which an organisation operates.

Corporate social responsibility (CSR) – The process by which an organisation minimises its negative impact and maximises its positive impact on society.

Decision-making unit – The team of people (usually in an organisation or family group) who make a buying decision.

Distribution – The 'Place' element of the marketing mix. Concerned with how the product or service reaches the end user based on the characteristics of the marketplace and the make-up of the product or service.

Ethics – A set of principles that take account of the moral aspects of decisions.

Extended marketing mix – A further 3Ps (People, Process and Physical Evidence) added to the marketing mix to take into account the unique nature of services and provide marketers with additional tactical options.

Fast-moving consumer goods (FMCG) – These include packaged food, beverages, toiletries and tobacco.

Intermediaries – People who promote the products or services of one company to another company or to end-consumers. They are sometimes referred to as 'middlemen'. Retailers and wholesalers are intermediaries.

Logistics – The physical distribution of products through the channel, including warehousing and transportation.

Macro environment – The external factors that affect companies' planning and performance, and that are beyond its control (PESTELE factors).

Market segmentation – The division of the market place into distinct sub-groups or segments, each characterised by particular shared tastes or interests and requiring a specific marketing mix.

Marketing mix – A mix of 4Ps (Product, Price, Promotion and Place), these are tactics a marketer can implement and adapt to meet the needs of key stakeholders. This has been further developed with the introduction of three additional Ps – see Extended Marketing Mix.

Media – The tools that can be used to deliver marketing messages – for example broadcast, digital, print and outdoor.

Message – A piece of communication that may contain a variety of signs, symbols and content that is designed to appeal to the audience and influence attitudes.

Micro environment – The immediate context of a company's operations, including its suppliers, customers and competitors.

Not-for-profit/third sector – The charity and voluntary sector. Objectives are different from those in commercial organisations, but marketing is still relevant.

Organisational buying decision-making process – The process that an organisation goes through when making a buying decision.

Relationship marketing – The strategy of establishing a relationship with the customer, which continues well beyond the first purchase.

Resources – The portfolio of assets owned or managed by an organisation.

Small to medium-sized enterprise (SME) – Usually defined as an organisation with fewer than 250 employees, with medium businesses having 50 to 249 employees and small businesses having up to 49 employees. Small businesses include micro businesses, which can be separately defined as having up to five employees.

Stakeholder – An individual or group that affects or is affected by the organisation and its operations.

FEEDBACK TO ACTIVITIES

ACTIVITY 1 (SEE P23)

Think about your own organisation and others that you know quite well. Make notes on:

- The extent to which they carry out market and customer research and how they use that information to improve the way they meet customer requirements. For example, how have they developed products and services over the past five years? What improvements have they made in response to changing customer needs or identified customer dissatisfaction?
- How effectively they communicate customer requirements across the organisation and how well people at every level understand them.
- The way they manage quality and how well people understand the need to satisfy both internal and external customers. Are suppliers included in the 'quality chain'?
- The importance attached to customer care. Are all staff trained effectively, or is it deemed to be the responsibility of front-line staff only?
- The willingness of people within the organisation to make changes for the customer or meet specific requirements that may not be routine. What part does marketing play in facilitating this change?

FEEDBACK

This will differ from organisation to organisation. You would be looking for:

- Continuous research being undertaken (for example, about customer satisfaction).
- Ad-hoc research being undertaken (for example, before new products are developed).
- Evidence of new product development or adjustments being made to products or services.
- Any internal marketing undertaken.
- Quality systems in place.
- Customer care systems and processes (for example complaint procedures).
- Staff training in customer service.
- Staff 'championing' the customer and making changes for their benefit.

ACTIVITY 2 (SEE P24)

Does your organisation have a marketing plan? If so, see how closely its content maps to the frameworks above. Make notes on areas that you feel are strengths and any gaps or weaknesses in the framework that could be improved.

FEEDBACK

This will differ from organisation to organisation. Most organisations do some form of planning, even if it is quite informal. However, you should look for evidence of the six main stages of the planning process:

- Situation analysis (or marketing audit).
- Objectives.
- Strategy.
- Tactics.
- Action or implementation.
- Control, monitoring or measurements.

If any of those stages are missing you should have notes on how improvements could be made by filling the gaps in the process.

ACTIVITY 3 (SEE P28)

Visit your favourite websites and identify the points that indicate customer focus. For example, how easy are they to navigate? What added value do they provide? Are there extra services, such as links to sources of helpful information?

FEEDBACK

This will depend on the websites you choose. As an example look at www.mini.co.uk. This contains the information you would expect in terms of the range, and the opportunity to request a brochure. You can easily navigate to any topic you want to investigate – servicing, accessories, booking a test drive, finding a dealership and so on.

In terms of additional information that adds value there is a 'Mini configurator' to help you design your own Mini, the opportunity to book a tour of the factory, details of the charity the company supports, and updates on its involvement in motor-sport.

ACTIVITY 4 (SEE P34)

If your organisation has a purchase and supply department, talk to them to find out what criteria they use to select appropriate suppliers.

If not, list the criteria you would like a printing firm that supplies you with marketing fliers, to meet.

FEEDBACK

Once again, this will vary depending on your organisation. However, you might have identified the following criteria for your list:

- How well do we know the firm? Have we used them before and how was that experience?
- Are they local?
- Will there be a single point of contact?
- What is the price?
- How soon can they deliver? Can they meet our deadline?
- How did they respond to our brief? Did they ask questions?
- How easy do we feel they would be to work with?

ACTIVITY 5 (SEE P47)

Your manager has asked you for a briefing paper that explains to staff in other departments the following elements of the macro environment, with an example factor from each:

- Social.
- Legal.
- Economic.
- Technological.

FEEDBACK

The examples you use will vary depending on the industry that you are in. An example is shown below:

Social	This group of factors includes demographics, lifestyles, social issues, education levels, attitudes and social trends.
	An example could be the ageing population, which might lead us to consider creating a mobile handset with bigger keys and is easier to operate.
Economic	This group of factors includes business cycles, inflation rates, unemployment levels and GNP trends.
	An example could be high unemployment, which means that although people still want mobile phones there is a trend towards pay-as- you-go arrangements rather than contracts.

Legal	This group of factors includes competition law, employment law, foreign trade regulation, environmental protection legislation and consumer protection legislation.
	An example could be that environmental protection legislation means we have to change the packaging that we currently use on our products to minimise damage to the environment.
Technological	This group of factors includes developments in technology, government investment in technology and product life cycles.
	An example could be that our main competitor is developing new products more quickly than we are and we need to develop our practices in order to take advantage of new developments in technology more quickly.

ACTIVITY 6 (SEE P48)

Your manager has asked you to prepare four slides for her to use in a short presentation to the board about the difference between ethics and social responsibility. Using PowerPoint, or a similar software package, produce the slides for the presentation.

FEEDBACK

ETHICS

Definition –

Moral philosophies that define right and wrong behaviour in marketing.

Important because they can have an impact on a company's reputation in a competitive marketplace.

Example of ethical behaviour

Researching and satisfying customer needs rather than creating needs.

SOCIAL RESPONSIBILITY

Definition –

An organisation's responsibility to minimise its negative impact on society as a whole, and maximise its positive impact, as far as is reasonably possible.

Example of social responsibility

A large supermarket planting trees after cutting some down to build a new store.

ACTIVITY 7 (SEE P49)

List five sources of information you could use to monitor the competitive environment in your own industry.

FEEDBACK

This will vary depending on your industry. An example might be:

- Websites of main competitors.
- Feedback from the sales force (from customers).
- Market intelligence reports.
- Press articles – for example, the *Financial Times*, the *Daily Telegraph*.
- Trade journals – for example, *The Grocer*, *Travel Trade Gazette*, *Construction News*.

ACTIVITY 8 (SEE P50)

List three key stakeholders of your organisation and make notes on the impact they have on the organisation and how marketing is used to communicate with them.

FEEDBACK

Your response may vary depending on the stakeholders you choose.

Stakeholder	Impact on organisation	Marketing communications used
Employees	High impact – need to present the brand to customers at all times.	Email, intranet.
Local community	High impact – get local support through communicating actively with community. We are a large employer locally.	Meetings, sponsorship of local charities.
Intermediaries	High impact – they are the face of our brand to many customers.	Sales force, extranet, email.

ACTIVITY 9 (SEE P60)

For an in-house marketing research training day with your team you have been asked to produce a handout that:

- Provides a list of clear examples of the different tools used to gather different types of marketing research.
- Describes the advantages and disadvantages of each example listed.

FEEDBACK

Handout – Market research in ABC Ltd

As you have seen in our training today, the following are the methods of research that we use, along with the advantages and disadvantages of each.

Method	Advantages	Disadvantages
Focus groups – a tool for marketing research where small groups of participants take part in guided discussions on the topic being researched.	Good for obtaining views and opinions of respondents. Group approach often means that one person's response sparks an idea with others.	Costly. Take time to arrange. Need professional moderating so that responses are honest and not 'led' by the organiser.
Online surveys.	Easy and quick to put together. Cheap to use. Can hit a wide audience.	Needs target group to be active online. No way of knowing how honest respondents are being.
Secondary research.	Cheap to do. Relatively quick to gather.	May not be available or accessible. May be out of date. Not originally collected for our purposes.

ACTIVITY 10 (SEE P64)

To be valuable, the information generated by an information system must fulfil certain criteria.

List the five criteria that make information valuable and, with reference to a source of information that your own marketing department uses, comment briefly on how well it meets those criteria.

FEEDBACK

In our marketing department we use reports from our in-house legal department. Information should be:

Relevant – Most of the information we have is relevant, although not always relevant specifically to marketing. Sometimes we have to pick out the information that is relevant to us, and it would be easier to use if this could be filtered before it is sent to us.

Complete – This is 85 per cent true. In some cases we have to ask questions about how parts of the information might affect us before we decide what action to take.

Accurate – Yes, this is always the case. The legal department is very careful to ensure the information is accurate, and this sometimes leads to delays.

Clear – Most of the time the information is clear. However, sometimes it contains legal jargon and we have to ask for an explanation.

Timely – See 'Accurate' above. Sometimes information is late reaching us. It seems to have been held back for further checks before it is issued.

ACTIVITY 11 (SEE P86)

A medium-sized furniture manufacturer that sells direct to its target market is looking to move from providing basic home furnishings to designing and producing bespoke, durable office furniture on a business-to-business basis. Complete the following table, comparing and contrasting the marketing mix for the existing consumer market and the proposed business-to-business market.

FEEDBACK

There would be some similarities but also key differences between the two different mixes for the furniture company. This is what we refer to as 'differentiated targeting'. Some identified differences are listed in the table.

	Home furnishings	Office furnishings
Product	Standardised furniture, basic design for use in the home.	Bespoke, durable, hard-wearing products for use in an office environment.
Price	Relatively cheap, competitive.	Negotiated, based on product specification.
Place	Sold direct to consumers online, distributed through key furniture retailers.	Sales team take product and ideas to the business customer.
Promotion	Significant online presence – via website and social media. Emailshots via CRM database. In-store advertising and sales promotions linked to older stock.	Personal selling is highly important, supported by direct marketing. Possible advertising in key business journals and relevant online channels.

ACTIVITY 12 (SEE P90)

Think about the last time you consumed a service rather than a tangible product. This may have been a visit to the cinema or theatre, or a sports event, or you may have been seeking advice about a financial issue.

Make notes on the marketing mix that is in place for this service, identifying all '7Ps'.

FEEDBACK

The activities identified for each of the 7Ps within the extended marketing mix would vary depending on the service experience identified and considered. However, if you used a visit to the cinema as an example, the notes may look something like this.

Product – **Core** – entertainment, escapism; **actual** – the film, audio and visual quality, comfort and environment; **augmented** – parking and access, concessions and snacks, service from staff.

Price – In line with rest of market, may be discounted for older film, premium for new release or blockbuster, further premium for VIP seats, variation depending on time of day.

Promotion – Advertisement and PR for film, email from cinema, online via website and social media, newspaper listings, sales promotions for cheaper tickets (advanced, special offers, loyalty rewards), personal selling (up-selling at retail concessions, for example).

Place – The cinema and the website.

People – Anyone you may interact with during the cinema experience – sales person (online or face to face), bar staff etc.

Process – Booking, paying for and collecting tickets, purchasing concessions (drinks, snacks and similar), finding the right screen and seat.

Physical evidence – Website or app, cinema foyer, seats and comfort, temperature, cleanliness.

ACTIVITY 13 (SEE P103)

How much do you know about internet advertising and the law, in particular data protection legislation covering the way personal information is stored and used?

Search on the internet for information that provides guidance to organisations on how to use digital communications to build relationships with customers.

FEEDBACK

The internet is difficult to regulate, particularly as it is a global medium and it is unclear under which country's laws an offender should be prosecuted. It isn't covered by broadcast legislation either, but advertisers should be aware of the codes of conduct set by the self-regulatory body the Advertising Standards Authority (ASA). Go to the section 'About ASA' on www.asa.org.uk to find out what rules to observe when designing advertisements.

You should also look at www.ico.org.uk – the website for the UK Information Commissioner's Office – to read about data protection rules.

But bear in mind that the law is changing constantly, so it's always advisable to seek specialist legal advice when publishing material in any medium.

ACTIVITY 14 (SEE P111)

Research ways that different organisations measure customer satisfaction. Make a list of the various methods used, and decide which would be the most appropriate for your organisation.

FEEDBACK

The most common ways of measuring customer satisfaction are:

- Surveys.
- Feedback cards.
- Monitoring social media.
- Number of complaints.

The one you choose will depend on the sector you work in, the size of your company and the nature of your customers.

REFERENCES

Kotler, P. *et al* (1997) *Marketing management: analysis, planning, implementation and control.* Prentice-Hall International.

Smith, P.R. (1993) *Marketing communications: an integrated approach.* London, Kogan Page.

Wilson, R.M.S. and Gilligan, C. (2005) *Strategic marketing management: planning, implementation and control.* Oxford, Elsevier Butterworth-Heinemann.

Rothaermal, F. (2012) *Strategic management: concepts and cases.* McGraw-Hill/Irwin.